Franz Werfel

FRANZ WERFEL
A photograph taken December 14, 1940 by Carl Van Vechten

Franz Werfel

1890-1945

EDITED BY LORE B. FOLTIN

UNIVERSITY OF PITTSBURGH
PRESS

©1961 by University of Pittsburgh Press
Library of Congress Catalog Card Number 61-7381

Printed in the United States of America by
Davis & Warde, Inc., Pittsburgh, Pa.

Preface

Many scholarly studies, in English as well as in German, concern themselves with such modern German writers as Rainer Maria Rilke and Franz Kafka, but there is a relative dearth of studies on their compatriot Franz Werfel.

The aim of this collection is to pay tribute to this writer whose work, in part at least, is readily available in translation to American readers. The writers of these essays, all American scholars—some with European backgrounds—approach the work of Werfel critically, yet with sympathetic understanding. Each essay forms an entity in itself, and it is my hope that the collection as a whole will contribute toward a deeper understanding and wider appreciation of Franz Werfel.

ACKNOWLEDGMENTS

To Alma Mahler Werfel, Franz Werfel's widow, I am profoundly grateful for her special permission to quote from Franz Werfel's hitherto unpublished correspondence. My most cordial thanks are due to Agnes Starrett, editor of the University of Pittsburgh Press, for her generous assistance in the final technical editing of the several essays. The interest in my work and the help of Dr. Alan C. Rankin, assistant chancellor for General Affairs, was of value to me. I am indebted to Carl Van Vechten, the author and critic, for the use of his photograph of Franz Werfel, which is published here for the first time, and to Blossom Henry Massey, associate professor emeritus, University of Pittsburgh, for her advice on questions of style. Charles W. Bangert of Miami University translated from the German the essay "Franz Werfel and the Stage."

I wish to thank *The German Quarterly* for permission to reprint the article by Adolf D. Klarmann, which appeared in Volume XXXII, 1959. For permission to adapt "Franz Werfel: Reporter of the Sublime" by

Heinz Politzer, I wish to thank *Commentary** where the original article was published in March 1950. Finally I am obliged to *The Kentucky Foreign Language Quarterly* for allowing me to use an expanded version of the article "Prague, a Background to Franz Werfel's Work" by Lore Barbara Foltin, published in Volume VII, 1960.

Lore B. Foltin
January, 1961

EDITORIAL NOTES

German titles mentioned in the essays have been translated into English in the first three chapters. In most of the subsequent essays only those titles appearing for the first time are translated. Unless another source is indicated in a footnote, each author is responsible for the English translation of quoted material. Any apparent discrepancies of dates may be due to the use of both writing and publication dates.

Contents

LORE BARBARA FOLTIN

Introduction: A Biography of Franz Werfel

Franz Werfel was born on September 10, 1890 in Prague. We do not know much of his ancestors, except that they belonged to the German Jewry of Bohemia. One of his forebears was a physician who practiced in the *Kleinseite* of Prague, one of the oldest sections of the city, located at the foot of the castle. His great-grandfather on his father's side served in the army of Napoleon during the Russian campaign. The son of this *Staabscourier* (high ranking messenger), who was to become Werfel's grandfather, came to Prague in the middle of the nineteenth century. He made enough money to allow him to send his child, Rudolph, Werfel's father, to a boarding school in Bavaria. But Fortune turned her back upon him and Rudolph Werfel, after his father's death, inherited mostly unpaid debts. He turned to the manufacture of gloves and amassed a small fortune.

When his son Franz was born, the family belonged to the wealthy upper middle class of Prague. Franz was the only son of the family, but he had two sisters. In the year 1957, Willy Haas, the "B.H." in Werfel's posthumously published last novel, *Stern der Ungeborenen (Star of the Unborn)*, and one of the most gifted of German critics, published a charming, moving, and witty book,[1] in which he describes the imposing

[1] *Die literarische Welt* (The Literary World), Paul List Verlag, München, 1957, p. 18.

In composing this brief biography of Franz Werfel, I relied heavily upon revelations of Franz Werfel himself, found in notes in his diaries which are deposited in the Werfel archive at the University of California in Los Angeles. Much of my information comes also from Dr. Gustave O. Arlt, Dean of the Graduate Division of the University of California, Werfel's long-time friend, his imaginative translator, and wise counselor. Dr. Arlt patiently answered my many questions. In consulting published biographical information, I was confronted with many discrepancies in the various histories of German literature and lexica. L.B.F.

residence of the Werfel family with wide, white corridors "in denen es immer irgendwie nach frischem Lack oder anderen Ingredienzien extrem vornehmer Sauberkeit roch." ("wherein there was always somehow a smell of fresh paint or other ingredients of extremely genteel cleanliness.")

Franz led a sheltered life and had a happy childhood which in no small measure was made so by his nurse whom he celebrated in many poems, and especially in his novel *Barbara oder Die Frömmigkeit (The Pure in Heart)*. He attended the well-known Piaristengymnasium, a type of high school which prepares for study at a university. After graduation he enrolled at the University of Prague (in 1909) to study law in preparation for the commercial career to which his father had destined him.

Much has been said about the antagonism that existed between Franz Werfel and his father. This father-son conflict found expression in such works as *Nicht der Mörder, der Ermordete ist schuldig (Not the Murderer . . .)* or *Spiegelmensch (Mirror Man)*, which were both published in 1920 and in a sense complement each other. Many critics find further proof of the hostile feelings which existed between parent and son in Franz's departure from home, in 1910, to work for a shipping company in Hamburg.[2] It must be borne in mind, however, that such conflict between father and son was a much used motif of Expressionism in German literature at that time, in which the sensitive younger generations are depicted as misunderstood by their authoritarian elders. We find it in Hasenclever's drama *Der Sohn (The Son*, 1913) and Kafka's story *Die Verwandlung (Metamorphosis*, 1916), to mention only two of the numerous examples. We cannot assume that all was harmonious between Werfel and his father, but to see in the former's works a direct reflection of an extremely unpleasant relationship would surely be to strain the facts.

The role of the father and of the son in his works is far more complicated. In the last analysis, the father represents God, the Father of mankind, the Lord of creation, while the son represents sometimes creation itself, sometimes human beings, sometimes the poet's self. In his relationship to the son, the father, which is to say, the Godhead, now appears as the loving parent, now as the stern giver of the law.[3]

[2] *Twentieth Century Authors*, ed. Stanley J. Kunitz and Howard Haycroft, The H. W. Wilson Co., New York, 1942, p. 1497.
[3] The meaning of the father-son relationship in Werfel's works is the theme of

In 1911 and 1912 Werfel served his year of compulsory military service. When it was over he did not resume formal studies at the university, but accepted a position in the young publishing firm of Kurt Wolff in Leipzig. Meanwhile, in 1911, he had published his first volume of poetry, *Der Weltfreund (Friend to the World)*, which had catapulted him overnight into fame and which established him as one of the great lyric poets of this century.

The war years, 1915-1917, Werfel spent first as a *Kanonier* (private) on the Italian front and later as a *Feuerwerker* (sergeant) in a regiment of artillery in Eastern Galicia. He felt, however, that life at the front held more than physical sufferings; the real hardships for him lay in the spirit of militarism which he detested and which prevailed in the barracks and in the lower military hierarchy.

Even during his years in the army, Werfel continued to write and to publish. By the time *Einander (To One Another)*, his third volume of poetry, appeared in 1915, he was hailed as the leader of Expressionism in German literature and its most exciting spokesman.

Toward the end of World War I, Werfel was arrested on a charge of high treason. He had been discharged from the army and had been living in Vienna since 1917, where his outspoken Pacifist views were found unbearable by the authorities.

That year he met a woman who was acknowledged the most beautiful in Vienna, Alma Maria Mahler, daughter of a painter and widow of the composer Gustav Mahler. The story of their courtship and marriage has been told by Alma Mahler Werfel herself in her book *And the Bridge is Love.*[4] It is the consensus among those who knew both Franz Werfel and his wife that she must be credited with much of his literary development and success.

During the comparatively peaceful years between the armistice of 1918 and the usurping of power by the Nazis in Austria in 1938, Werfel lived the life of the Viennese intellectual elite with the usual journeys abroad. These led him to Germany, Switzerland, Czechoslovakia, his native country, to Italy, Palestine, Egypt, and even to far-off America. Those who remember his appearance on a radio program "I'm an American," sponsored by the Department of Justice during World War II,

Bernhard Maier's doctoral dissertation *Vater und Sohn. Zur Deutung der Dichtung Franz Werfels* (Father and Son. An Interpretation of Franz Werfel's Poetic Work), Freiburg im Breisgau, 1959.

[4] Harcourt, Brace and Company, New York, 1958.

were moved by his nostalgic identification of himself with Vienna, the native city of Schubert and the adoptive city of Haydn, Mozart, and Beethoven. Werfel saw in the compositions of these great musicians a true expression of the humanistic Viennese atmosphere.

Franz Werfel, who had started writing as a lyric poet, became a highly successful dramatist during the era following World War I. One of his earliest dramas, *Die Troerinnen (The Trojan Women)*, an adaptation of Euripides' play, which first appeared in the *Weiße Blätter* in 1914, had more than 50 performances in Berlin in 1916. But it was *Juarez und Maximilian* with its splendid portrayal of the Hapsburgian Emperor of Mexico, published in 1924, which brought him fame as a dramatist. The *Akademie der Wissenschaften* (Academy of Science) in Vienna announced to him in a letter of January 18, 1926, the award of the Grillparzer prize for the play. The holograph manuscript of *Juarez und Maximilian* is deposited in the *Österreichische Nationalbibliothek* (National Library of Austria). It is the only handwritten document this library holds of Werfel's writing.

In his middle years, Werfel consciously turned his attention to the popular literary form of the novel. It is not surprising that his first full-length novel is *Verdi. Roman der Oper (Verdi, A Novel of the Opera)*, for Werfel was a lifelong devotee of the Italian master. Two years later, in 1926, he adapted the Italian libretto of Verdi's *La Forza del Destino (The Power of Fate)* for the German operatic stage, under the same title: *Die Macht des Schicksals*. It was the first of the three librettos of Verdi's operas which Werfel freely translated from the Italian. He also edited Verdi's letters.

Werfel's first truly international success came in 1933 with the publication of *Die vierzig Tage des Musa Dagh (The Forty Days of Musa Dagh)* which deals with the cruel treatment the inhabitants of several Armenian villages received at the hands of the Turks. By an ironic turn of fate, this same year, 1933, which marks the ascent to power by Hitler, is the year in which the Prussian *Kultusminister* (cultural secretary) ordered the expulsion of Werfel from the *Akademie der Künste* (Academy of Arts).[5] Werfel surely considered this stupid act rather an honor than an insult, for among the others expelled from the academy were Thomas Mann, Alfred Döblin, and Georg Kaiser, whereas the great poet Stefan George declined the invitation to become a member,

[5] Walter A. Berendsohn, *Die humanistische Front* (The Humanistic Front), Europa Verlag, Zürich, 1946, p. 23.

and Ricarda Huch, historian and poetess, gave up her membership.

When the Nazis overran Austria in 1938, Franz Werfel was away from home. He was never to return. If the thought of never again seeing his summer home in Breitenstein on the Semmering near Vienna saddened him, the fate of Austria was an almost unbearable tragedy to him. When the news reached him he was ill, and later on he felt this illness to be almost a blessing: for in his feverish state the ghastly truth only slowly penetrated his consciousness.

For the two following years he and his wife lived in an old mill in Sanary-sur-mer in Southern France where he wrote the novel *Der veruntreute Himmel (Embezzled Heaven)*. It is the first of Werfel's novels to hold his delightful humor. The figure of Teta who has been cheated out of heaven by her fraudulent nephew has in its fullness few equals in German literature.[6]

When France fell and the Franco-German armistice was signed, the Werfels, realizing the precariousness of their position as old foes of totalitarianism, fled from the ever advancing German forces. They shared the suffering of countless other refugees. They waited in consular offices in the hope of receiving the coveted visa to America, and finally made a desperate attempt at crossing the Pyrenees on foot into Spain. For a time, they found refuge and consolation in Lourdes, where Werfel's famous vow was made: If it should be granted to him to reach the shores of America, he would set aside work on everything else to sing the "Song of Bernadette," the little peasant girl who saw the vision of a beautiful lady in the grotto of Massabielle near Lourdes.

After much anguish and travail—having in exasperation even destroyed some of his manuscripts lest they fall into the hands of the Nazis—he and his wife made their way to a Greek ship, the Nea Hellas, and reached America and safety. They settled in California, where at that time there already existed a veritable colony of European writers and artists: Thomas Mann, Bruno Frank, Bruno Walter, and others.

In fulfillment of his vow, Werfel wrote *Das Lied von Bernadette (The Song of Bernadette)*. It was his greatest popular success, and like *Embezzled Heaven,* a Book-of-the-Month Club selection. Its filmed version started the career of the actress Jennifer Jones, and won five Academy awards.

[6] Paul Stöcklein "Franz Werfel" in *Deutsche Literatur im zwanzigsten Jahrhundert* (German Literature in the Twentieth Century), Hermann Friedemann and Otto Mann, editors, Wolfgang Rothe Verlag, Heidelberg, 1954, p. 272.

The fall of France and the subsequent flight of the refugees from the terrors of the Nazis furnished the background to Werfel's play *Jacobowsky und der Oberst (Jacobowsky and the Colonel)*, the inimitable "Komödie einer Tragödie" ("Comedy of a Tragedy") as the subtitle says. The American public saw this play in an adaptation by Sam N. Behrman. Its success was tremendous. The original German play, as Werfel wrote it, appeared first as a college text, edited by Dr. Gustave O. Arlt. "Literary history will note the unusual, and perhaps unique, fact that the first edition of a significant German book appeared in the shape of a text edition for American students," Dr. Arlt states in his preface.[7]

By the time *Jacobowsky and the Colonel* was playing to capacity audiences, Werfel was a sick man and he knew that his days were numbered. Ill health forced him to decline many invitations to appear as the featured speaker before various groups. Fortunately, he was able to accept in person the honorary degree of Doctor of Laws which he was awarded by the University of California on June 9, 1943. In the citation he was lauded as a "novelist, playwright, and lyric poet, fertile in imagination and skilled in the use of language—tolerant and understanding of human nature, unflagging in optimism as to the dignity and destiny of man—an author whose writings passing over the confines of geography, are today widely read in England, France, and the United States, and some day will be prized in Germany."

While finishing *Stern der Ungeborenen (Star of the Unborn)*, Werfel often had his private physician stay in the house with him. For long periods of time he slept with an oxygen tent beside his bed. Most of *Star of the Unborn*, considered by some critics his masterpiece, was written at a cottage he rented from the El Mirasol Hotel in Santa Barbara, California, which afforded him the "quietness of a monastery" that he thought essential to the creative process. When the novel was published, Werfel was no longer living. The end came in August 1945, shortly before his fifty-fifth birthday, at his home on North Bedford Drive in Beverly Hills, California, while he was making final revisions of his *Gedichte aus den Jahren 1908-1945 (Poems from the Years 1908-1945)*.

Even though rumors of his deathbed conversion to the Catholic faith persisted, Werfel died a Jew. He was given a Catholic burial by a special dispensation of the Archbishop of the Los Angeles diocese.

[7] Appleton-Century-Crofts, New York, 1945, p. iii.

Werfel, one of the great novelists and dramatists of today, will probably live on in history, especially to the German-speaking peoples, as one of the outstanding lyric poets of the twentieth century. Paul Wiegler, German critic and essayist, called him "den Mozart der neuen Lyrik"[8] ("the Mozart of the new lyric poetry"). No finer compliment could be paid him, to whom music was always a source of deepest inspiration.

[8] Quoted in Wilhelm Herzog's *Menschen, denen ich begegnete* (People I have met), Francke Verlag, Bern und München, 1959, p. 458.

LORE BARBARA FOLTIN

Prague: Background to Franz Werfel's Work

Prague is a city where for centuries Germans, Czechs, and Jews have lived together. It is an old city. Over its crooked streets hover the legends of its mythical foundress, Libussa. Its dark Gothic doorways reeked of old of the smelting pots of alchemists in their quest for gold. Its Renaissance windows look out upon the stories of John Huss. Its gorgeous baroque palaces recall the lavish balls of centuries. It is the city of Rabbi Loew and his *golem*, his robot; of the great scientist Tycho de Brahe; and of Wallenstein, the celebrated general. Meyrink's occult stories are laid there, and there was first heard the gay music of the *Bartered Bride*. Black magic was frequently practiced; cool stone churches tower over the city's medieval roofs. And the University of Prague, founded in 1348, is the oldest university in central Europe.

In this city Franz Werfel was born in 1890 of wealthy Jewish parents. Here young Franz grew up; here he wrote his first poems. And even though Werfel, like his older countryman Rilke, left Praque in his youth and returned only for infrequent visits, he never forgot the "city of a hundred steeples." He evokes its sights and smells and atmosphere for us in his work—indeed the very first poem Werfel published was "Die Gärten der Stadt Prag" ("The Gardens of Prague").[1]

The Jews of Prague were German-speaking, but around them there was no German national community. They were closely surrounded by Czechs. The nearest Germans lived in the Sudetenland, and farther away others inhabited "cultural islands" in Moravia. It is therefore not surprising that the literature of the Prague writers in the German tongue

[1] It was printed in the Viennese *Zeit* (Time). Willy Haas tells of this happy moment in his book *Die literarische Welt*, Paul List Verlag, München, 1957, p. 19. "Zum ersten Mal war Franz Werfel gedruckt! . . . In einer plötzlichen großen inneren Bewegung fielen wir einander fast weinend in die Arme." (For the first time Franz Werfel was printed! . . . In a sudden great inward emotion we fell into each others arms, almost crying.)

8

was a literature of the city, for whenever they reached beyond their own group, they touched upon Czech soil and culture.

Pavel Eisner, in his book *Franz Kafka and Prague*,[2] states that to understand Kafka truly one must have a knowledge of his city of Prague: its history, its politics, and the various national groups of which its population was composed. In my judgment, this is true of all the writers of the "Prague school," Rilke, Kafka, Werfel, Johannes Urzidil, and Max Brod. It was Max Brod who coined the expression "Prague school," meaning that certain conditions which existed nowhere else but in Prague shaped decisively the creative genius of these writers. All of them were born there in the late nineteenth century and spent their youth there on the Moldau, and all of them are trying "to see the world in its connection with the transcendental and the metaphysical."[3] The Prague influence, long neglected by critics and interpreters of literature, until Pavel Eisner pointed it out in his brilliant essay, has since been recognized. Peter Demetz in *René Rilkes Prager Jahre (René Rilke's Prague Years)* bases his interpretation of the poet's work and life upon a thorough study of the unique Prague milieu.[4] Willy Haas, childhood friend of Kafka, Brod, and Werfel, recreates in *Die Literarische Welt* the world of Prague as it existed in the waning years of the Austrian Empire, the world that Franz Werfel immortalized in *An Essay upon the Meaning of Imperial Austria.* Recently the writers of the "Prague school" have returned in their work to their native city. Max Brod's novel *Rebellische Herzen*[5] *(Rebellious Hearts)* and his story *Jugend im Nebel*[6] *(Youth in the Fog)* give evidence of such a return, as does Johannes Urzidil's *Die verlorene Geliebte*[7] *(The Lost Beloved).* These books are filled with the writers' love of Prague as they knew it before dictatorial powers changed its face.

[2] Arts, Inc., New York, 1950.

[3] Taken from a letter which Brod wrote to me concerning an introduction to his story "Der Tod ist ein vorübergehender Schwächezustand" (Death is a Passing State of Weakness) which is included in my collection *Aus Nah und Fern,* Houghton Mifflin Co., Boston, 1950.

[4] Eugen Diederichs Verlag, Düsseldorf, 1953, p. 6. "Rilkes Leben und Arbeit ist weit mehr, als es seinen eigenen Angaben nach den Anschein hätte, von seiner persönlichen Antwort auf die *Herausforderung des Ortes und der Zeit seiner Herkunft* [my italics] bestimmt." (Rilke's life and work is far more affected by his personal answer to the *challenge of his time and his place of origin* [my italics] than would appear from his own statements.

[5] F. A. Herbig, Berlin-Grunewald, 1957.

[6] Eckart Verlag, Berlin, 1959.

[7] Albert Langen-Georg Müller, München, 1956.

Franz Werfel's work is rooted deeply in Prague, and the city's people, landmarks, and spiritual and intellectual climate pervade his writings with their distinctive atmosphere.

In the novel, *Der Abituriententag (Class Reunion)*, the city is not specifically named, but it is easily guessed by those who know Prague. In another novel, *Der veruntreute Himmel (Embezzled Heaven)*, the parish church of Straschnitz is mentioned and the crisis occurs in the tenement district of Prague, inaptly called the "New World." Werfel describes this tenement as near the military barracks: "Baufälliges Winkelwerk von Häusern drängt sich hier wie auf Abbruch. Versehentlich hat die weit ins Land hinauszielende Entwicklung der Stadt diesen Moder links liegenlassen, mit seinen schiefen Dächern, wurmstichigen Loggien, schmutzigen Höfchen und ausgetretenen Holzstiegen." ("A tortuous congeries of dilapidated buildings seems to be waiting for the house-wrecker. The city has spread far out into what was once the countryside, having forgotten this quarter and left it to moulder away with its crooked roofs, worm-eaten loggias, squalid little courts, and worn wooden steps.")[8] In contrast to the ugly immediate surroundings, the view from the room where the heroine confronts her guilty nephew is beautiful, even in these cheap quarters. "Im Fenster . . . drängt sich eine schöne Aussicht zusammen, ein Gewirr altertümlicher Dächer und Giebel, von schwebenden Blütenkronen unterbrochen, und dahinter im bläulichen Gespensterreich die Kuppeln und Türme Mütterchen Prags wie Nebelbilder." ("Through the window, a beautiful view crowds together, a jumble of ancient roofs and gables, punctuated by soaring tree-crowns in full bloom, and behind, in the bluish ghost-realm, like misty images stand the domes and towers of Mother Prague.") Werfel, and also the other writers from Prague, speak of "Mütterchen Prag." Actually, the connotation is not German, but Slavic. No writer from Germany refers to a city as "Mütterchen." It is a direct translation from the Czech *matečka Praha*. In the short story *Weißenstein, der Weltverbesserer (Weißenstein, the World Reformer)* we read: "Unsere Geschichte beginnt in einem dieser Cafés.[9] Es lag an einer Straßenecke des geheimnisvollen Prag, dieser Stadt der großen Türme, der schweren

[8] This translation comes from Moray Firth (pseudonym), The Viking Press, New York, 1940, p. 213.

[9] Werfel refers here to the "Café Arco" where the literary circle of the youthful Prague writers met. Johannes Urzidil mentions this coffeehouse, together with Werfel, Kafka, and Weißenstein, the world reformer, in *Die verlorene Geliebte*, pp. 110, 111.

Schatten und ausgesuchten Sonderlage." ("Our story begins in one of these coffeehouses. It was situated on a street corner of the mysterious city of Prague, this city of great towers, heavy shadows, and peculiarly odd location.") Other descriptions occur in "Das Trauerhaus" (The House of Mourning"): for example, in the opening chapter mention is made of the dancing school which "Herr Pirik in einem schöen Barockpalais nahe der berühmten Brücke etabliert hatte." ("Mr. Pirik had established in a beautiful baroque palace near the famous bridge.") The bridge is the ancient Karlsbrücke that young René Rilke, before he determined to conquer the literary world as Rainer Maria, charmingly sings of in one of his rare humorous moods:

> Aber diese Nepomucken!
> Von des Torgangs Lucken gucken
> und auf allen Brucken sprucken
> lauter, lauter Nepomucken![10]

(But these Nepomucks! From the doorway they look out, and on all the bridges appear ghosts of many, many Nepomucks.)

In his own poems, Werfel evokes the city of his birth, the Prague of the old Austrian Monarchy in his *Ballade vom Winterfrost,* and in *Eine Prager Ballade,* the Prague that was overrun by the Nazis. In a train, traveling in America, the poet falls asleep and dreams. The old Czech coachman, Mr. Wáwra, is driving the horses to get home to Prague quickly. But Werfel reminds him in anguish that his parents' home is surrounded by Nazis. The dream has turned into a nightmare.

Many names and characters in Werfel's work reveal the influence of his early years spent in Prague. There is the chief protagonist of the novel *Barbara (The Pure in Heart),* the compassionate one, who guards his sleep, whose love passes understanding. Her nickname, Babi is, in the Czech language, a diminutive for "grandmother." Barbara, Ferdinand's nurse, is like a mother to the orphan, always appearing on the scene at the moment of his greatest need. In her Werfel has erected a memorial to his old nurse, Babi. Then there is Krasny, the poet in the same novel, whose name means "beautiful" in Czech. In *Der veruntreute Himmel,* the heroine is Teta, the shrewd and yet lovable cook: Teta means "aunt" in the Czech language. Teta is an old woman of typical Slavic physiognomy "mit breiten Backenknochen" ("with broad cheekbones"), who speaks "mit einem harten slawischen Tonfall" ("with a

[10] Rainer Maria Rilke, *Gedichte,* Insel Verlag, Leipzig, 1933, p. 49.

hard Slav intonation"). She likes to sing and still has "die kühle und klare Stimme eines Jungmädchens" ("the cool and clear voice of a young girl"). Like Barbara, Teta is neither educated nor a person with a high I.Q., but she has a distinct personality and she knows more about what Werfel often called the last questions than do the intelligentsia. When young Philipp dies, she is the only one in the household "die mit dem Tode auskam" ("who was on good terms with death"). This death, like all deaths, is to her an entrance into Paradise.

Yes, Werfel's work is peopled with Slavs. In the short story "Das Trauerhaus" we meet lieutenant Kohout (the "rooster") and Ludmilla and Nejedli; there are Slav names in the drama *Bocksgesang (Goat Song);* or one might mention the many Czech names in the stirring drama about the Hussite movement, *Das Reich Gottes in Böhmen (God's Kingdom in Bohemia).*

Even more revealing of the role that Prague played in Werfel's life are his personal remarks, not intended for publication, such as those we find in his letters to Alma Mahler, the widow of the composer, his Muse, who later became his wife. In the Werfel archive at the University of California at Los Angeles are seven colored photographs on postcards that Werfel sent to his future wife in Vienna while he was visiting his family in Prague. All are dated 1919. One showing the evening light over the castle with the *Kleinseite*[11] reads, "An dieser Abendstimmung ist nichts gefälscht, außer daß es in Wirklichkeit noch magischer ist. Alpenglühen auf einem Domgebirge." ("In this evening mood, nothing is false save that the reality of it is still more magical. The last reflection of the sun gilds the cathedral roofs.") Another card again depicts the *Kleinseite:* "Ich sende Dir Ansichtskarten aus Prag, damit Du siehst wie göttlich schön die längstvergessene Gestalt dieser Stadt ist." ("I am sending you picture postcards from Prague that you may see how divinely beautiful is the long-forgotten image of this city.") In a letter from Prague, dated 1933, he writes, ". . . Ich gehe viel spazieren. Das tut mir wohl. Die alte Stadt ist so geheimnisvoll und weltfern. Ähnlich wie Venedig. . . ." ("I take many walks. They do me good. The old city, like Venice, is mysterious and secluded.")[12]

Werfel lived a great part of his life in Austria, in Italy, in France, and during his last years, in America; yet as late as 1943, two years

[11] A section of Prague. Goethe's friend, Kaspar Graf Sternberg, lived here.
[12] I am greatly indebted to Mrs. Alma Mahler Werfel for special permission to quote from Franz Werfel's unpublished letters.

before his untimely death, he nostalgically remembers the *Stadtpark* (city park) of Prague. In his poem "Sechs Setterime zu Ehren des Frühlings von Neunzehnhundertundfünf" ("Six Stanzas in Honor of the Spring of 1905"), devoted to the memory of the actress of Schiller's plays, Maria Immisch, our poet muses:

> Der Stadtpark war schon dicht belaubt.
> Der Flieder rief . . .

(The city park was already in full leaf. The lilacs called . . .)

The city park is a memory of his childhood for Werfel, and it, as well as an elderly woman, usually of lowly status, appear in many of his poems. In *Der Weltfreund (Friend to the World)* we read:

> Ich bin wie nach dem Regen
> Der Stadtpark vor dem Haus . . .

(I am like the city park in front of the house after a rain . . .)

In the collection *Wir sind (We Are)*, there is the poem that brought Werfel to the attention of Joachim Maass[13] which begins:

> Eine alte Frau geht wie ein runder Turm
> Durch die alte Hauptallee im Blättersturm . . .

(Like a round tower, an old woman walks through the old broad avenue in a storm of leaves . . .)

The Germans of Prague lived in a kind of ghetto, surrounded as they were by Czechs, a people who spoke another language and were of a different culture. The German children of Prague were brought up by Czech nurses, served at table by Czech servants, had their clothes fitted by Czech seamstresses, rode on streetcars driven by Czech motormen. But they went to German schools—Rilke, Kafka, Brod, Willy Haas, and Franz Werfel all went to the German Piaristengymnasium—read German newspapers, such as the liberal *Prager Tagblatt* or the more chauvinistic *Bohemia,* had their own German theaters and clubs, such as the *Deutches Haus* in the choice location of the brilliant avenue, the *Graben,* and spoke German at home and with their friends.

The German they spoke, however, was neither the rich, expressive idiom of Germany nor the sweet, musical, nonchalant German of Aus-

---

[13] Maass later wrote the beautiful eulogy "Das begnadete Herz" (The Favored Heart), *Die Stockholmer Neue Rundschau,* II, 1946, and admirably grasped the essence of Werfel's greatness.

tria; it was an impoverished language, that language of the upper class
Prague Germans, interwoven with Czech expressions, and among the
Jews, with some words of Yiddish.[14] This peculiar language in which
Czech words are mixed quite naturally with German can be illustrated
by many early poems of Rilke. The following quotation is from "Der
kleine Dratenik" ("The Little Tinker"). Here, even in the title, the
mixture of language can be observed. Only a writer from Prague could
choose such a title. A German from Germany or Austria would, of
course, have called the poem "Der kleine Drahtbinder." In an appar-
ently effortless way, Czech and German words rhyme with each other:

> 'Nur einen Krajcar, nur einen
> für ein Stück Brot, milost' pánků!'
> Da!—Und er stammelt mir Dank zu,
> doch läßt nicht Ruh er den Beinen.[15]

(Just a penny, just one, for a bit of bread, Sir! There! And he stammers his
thanks as his legs jump up and down.)

The word *Krajcar* is a corruption of the German *Kreuzer* (penny).
Such corruptions were quite common in Prague, in both languages—
that is, the Czechs used German words, creating a language popularly
called *Kuchelböhmisch* (kitchen-Czech)—from *Kuchel,* a corruption of
die Küche (kitchen), because this language evolved in the kitchen in
conversations between the German *Herrschaft* (master and mistress)

---

[14] Compare Willy Haas, *Die literarische Welt*, p. 10. "Die Juden sprachen
Deutsch und waren österreichische Patrioten . . . Die höhere Beamtenschaft
sprach ein völlig denaturalisiertes, steriles und groteskes k.u.k. Tschechisch-
deutsch. Die Adeligen in ihren geheimnisvollen, riesigen Barockpalästen auf der
Kleinseite sprachen Französisch und gehörten keiner Nation an, sondern dem
Heiligen Römischen Reich, das es seit fast einem Jahrhundert nicht mehr gab."
(The Jews spoke German and were Austrian patriots . . . The higher officials
spoke a completely unnatural, sterile, grotesque, Royal-Imperial Czech-German.
The aristocracy, in their mysterious, gigantic, baroque palaces on the *Kleinseite,*
spoke French and belonged to no actual nation but instead to the Holy Roman
Empire, which had not existed for almost a century.) Similarly, and humorously,
Johannes Urzidil, *Die verlorene Geliebte,* p. 40. " . . . denn in Prag, von wo ich
kam, redete man das Hochdeutsch der Kanzlei des Kaisers Karl IV." (. . . for in
Prague, where I came from, one spoke the High German of the chancellery of
Emperor Charles IV.) Or, p. 75. "Es war ein übernationales Deutsch und als
solches symbolisch für den völkerverbindenden Charakter der Österreichisch-
Ungarischen Monarchie." (It was a supra-national German and as such symbolic
of the character of the Austro-Hungarian Monarchy which made all its peoples
one.)

[15] Rilke, *Gedichte,* p. 98.

and the Czech servants. On the other hand, the Germans of Prague did not hesitate to Germanize many Czech words and use them in their peculiar *Prager Deutsch* (Prague German). In the poem cited above, *milost' pánků* rhyming with *Dank zu* is a Czech diminutive corresponding to the German *gnädiger Herr.* Rilke also does not mind rhyming the German *ihm* with the Czech *Prosím,* meaning "please." Franz Kafka demonstrates the Slavic influence by using *bis* in the sense of "as soon as," which is a Germanized form of the Czech *až,*—a native German would say, of course, *sobald.*[16] Franz Werfel has some of this *Lokal-kolorit* (local color) in his work, for instance: ". . . ich fahre Sie *auf*[17] Prag." ("I am driving you to Prague.") Or: "Far ich Sie *stantepe*[18] übers Atlantische Meer." ("I'll whip you this instant across the Atlantic.")

The peculiar situation existing in Prague made life difficult for the German writers of the city, since they were creating in a sort of vacuum. In time, they all found a wider reading public. They did this by moving to Vienna, to Munich, to Berlin. None of them felt drawn to their Sudeten-German compatriots, upon whom they looked with a mixture of disgust and envy: with disgust, because the German writers of the Sudetenland were unsophisticated, rather coarse, politically biased and epigonal; with envy, because these Sudeten-Germans had their roots in the soil, they lived in a German-speaking environment, amidst the serene beauty of the Erzgebirge and the Riesengebirge. And yet, the literature of the German Sudetenland remained provincial, whereas the work of the city-bred writers such as Rilke and Werfel was destined to become world literature.[19]

[16] Also pointed out by Pavel Eisner, *Franz Kafka and Prague,* p. 95.

[17] My italics.

[18] Ditto.

[19] Peter Demetz, *René Rilkes Prager Jahre,* p. 108. It is interesting to note in this connection Oskar Schürer, *Prag,* Georg D. W. Callwey Verlag und Rudolf M. Rohrer Verlag, München-Brünn, 1935, p. 354. "Die Deutschen in Prag waren von je soziale Oberschicht. In früheren Jahrhunderten war diese deutsche Ober-schicht von einem kräftigen Handwerkerstand getragen worden. Der war in neueren Zeiten teils durch Abwanderung, teils durch Aufgehen in den oberen Ständen, teils aber auch durch Aufsaugung durch die tschechischen Mittelklassen immer mehr abgeschmolzen. Ergänzender Zuzug vom Lande her fehlte. Der Zustrom tschechischer Landbevölkerung füllte die Fabriken, ließ Deutsche kaum mehr zu. . . . da stand das Prager Deutschtum einsam zwischen fremdem Volks-tum, eine Gesellschaft gebildeter Geister unter sich. Lebendige Volkskraft gedieh nicht mehr in solcher Luft. Wohl aber in manchen Kreisen eine erlesene Spätkultur, der dann ein Rainer Maria Rilke aus frühen Erlebnissen, die er hier aufgenommen hatte, in seiner Dichtung die Verklärung schuf." (Ever since, the

The majority of German citizens of Prague considered themselves a part of the "ruling" classes, but those among them who became writers felt a brotherly love for their Czech countrymen. Hence, the many Czech motives in this German literature, for example, Rilke's fascination with Dalibor, the Czech knight, or with Joseph Kajetan Týl, the Czech actor-poet of the prerevolutionary period, the *Vormärz*, whose haunting song of peace, "Kde domov můj," ("Where my home is") was to become the National anthem of the Czechoslovak Republic. When Rilke visited the *Národopisná výstava,* an ethnographic exhibit which showed the reconstructed room of the Czech patriot, he conceived the poem:

> Da also hat der arme Týl
> sein Lied 'Kde domov můj' geschrieben.
> In Wahrheit: Wen die Musen lieben,
> dem gibt das Leben nicht zuviel.[20]

(That is where poor Týl wrote his song, "Where my home is." In truth, to him whom the Muses love, life does not freely give much.)

The political significance of these lines of the young Rilke are not immediately apparent today. The Prague German press ignored the Czech exhibit. No German condescended to visit the exhibition grounds. In contrast to this ethnic snobbery, a typical case of sour grapes on the part of many Germans who narrow-mindedly could not endure the surging vitality of the Czechs, Rilke braved the public opinion of the Germans and not only visited the exhibit, but also published the poem.[21]

He was not alone in this public expression of brotherly love toward the Czechs. A few years later Max Brod translated the texts of Leoš Janáček's operas into German and was instrumental in introducing this

---

Germans of Prague had belonged to the upper classes. In former times, this German upper stratum had been supported by a vigorous class of artisans, but in more modern times, this working group had more and more melted away, partly because of emigration, partly by rising into the upper social classes, and partly through absorption by the Czech middle classes. Replenishing migration of artisans from the country was lacking. The influx of Czech population from there filled the factories, hardly admitting Germans any longer. . . . there stood the Prague German nationals, lonely amid a foreign people, a society of educated minds by themselves. Living folk-vigor no longer thrived in such an atmosphere, but what did thrive in some circles was an elevated late culture which Rainer Maria Rilke, for example, from his early experiences here, transfigured in his poetic work.)

[20] Rilke, *Gedichte,* p. 60.   [21] Demetz, *René Rilkes Prager Jahre,* p. 145.

ultra-Czech music to Germany. Franz Kafka attached himself to Milena Jesenká, a Czech woman. Franz Werfel translated poems of the Czech writer Ottakar Březina. In a letter to Alma Mahler from Prague, dated 1921, Werfel writes: "Spreche niemanden außer dem tschechischen Dichter Dvořák,[22] der einen großen Eindruck auf mich macht. Eine wirkliche Natur! Ein Mann!—Er will den "Bocksgesang," in den er ganz verliebt ist, für die Bühne hier einrichten und übersetzen." ("I see none except the Czech poet Dvořák, who impresses me greatly. A real person! A man!—He completely fell in love with *Goat Song*, which he plans to arrange for the stage here and wants to translate.")

So Werfel, like the others, broke out of the vacuum by making friends with Czech writers; he, too, moved away from Prague and cut the umbilical cord, but while the influence of his new environment and the freedom of expression it brought in its train cannot be overlooked, the real liberation was subjective. I refer to Werfel's faith which he summed up in the preface to *Das Lied von Bernadette (The Song of Bernadette)* in the mellifluous words: "Schon in den Tagen, da ich meine ersten Verse schrieb, hatte ich mir zugeschworen immer und überall durch meine Schriften zu verherrlichen das göttliche Geheimnis und die menschliche Heiligkeit . . . ." ("Even in the days when I wrote my first verses I vowed that I would evermore and everywhere in all I wrote magnify the divine mystery and the holiness of man."[23]) That need for adoration of the Unseen Reality, that yearning to draw nearer to the Divine[24] which made Werfel the eloquent champion of faith that he is, seems to have its origin in the city of massive church towers and lofty spires, the ancient city of Prague. That need and desire run like a scarlet thread through his work. "Die eigentliche historische Erbschaft, die diese Stadt ihren Dichtern vermachte, war die mystische Ekstase." ("The real historical legacy, which this city left to her poets, was the mystical ecstasy.") So states Peter Demetz, and he continues, "Unter den hundert Glockentürmen geriet jedes Gefühl in die gefährliche Nähe religiöser Verzückung."[25] ("Under the hundred bell towers every

[22] Arno Dvořak, Czech author, (1881-1933).

[23] *The Song of Bernadette,* translated by Ludwig Lewisohn, The Viking Press, New York, 1942, p. 7.

[24] For a different point of view, see Heinz Politzer, "Prague and the origins of Rainer Maria Rilke, Franz Kafka, and Franz Werfel," *Modern Language Quarterly,* XVI, 1955, p. 5. "The poet of the Slavic-Christian revolution settled down as a eulogist of the Austrian restoration, a pseudo-Catholic poet."

[25] *René Rilkes Prager Jahre,* p. 108.

feeling approached the dangerous neighborhood of religious rapture.")

This mystical yearning burns, an inextinguishable flame, in our poet's heart. It is imparted to his characters in a variety of ways, sometimes subtle, sometimes straightforward, sometimes complex, and then again with childlike simplicity; but it is always there, triumphant over the base or the mere materialistic. We find it in Barbara, whose faith is like a rock. We find it in Teta, who has arranged her whole life with a view to the hereafter. We find it in Bernadette's unshakable belief in and the sublime rapture of her love for the lady of her visions. It is the basic theme of Werfel's essays, dramas, and poetry.

Thus, in spite of his wanderings, Werfel remained a child of Prague. Even in his final novel, *Stern der Ungeborenen (Star of the Unborn)*, which takes place in an imaginary region and in the far-distant future, there are many reminiscences of Prague: ". . . obwohl ich jetzt mit Heimweh an die Türe und Tore unserer mittelalterlichen Heimatstadt denken muß, an ihre Hochburg, den Hradschin, an ihre gotischen und barocken Paläste." (". . . although I get homesick when I think of the towers and gates of our medieval city back home, its stronghold, the Hradschin, its Gothic and baroque palaces."[26]) Not just the castle, the Hradschin, rises before the reader, but also the Wyschehrad, Prague's oldest fortress at the southern edge of the city, and the Ufergasse, the quai on the river, play their parts in the story. Werfel, the cosmopolitan, never lost his love for the city of his childhood.

[26] *Star of the Unborn*, translated by Gustave O. Arlt, The Viking Press, New York, 1946, p. 17.

HEINZ POLITZER

Franz Werfel: Reporter of the Sublime

In 1948 Erich Kahler, humanist and arbiter of German letters, re-
viewed Franz Werfel's *Poems 1908-1945*. His critique was more than
an evaluation of Werfel's lyrical gifts; it amounted to an assessment of
the poet's entire personality. Werfel, he said, "was a bad author and a
great poet. This is rare enough in itself. But even rarer is the deep connection between the two. His novels and plays show neither the spon-
taneous purity of a genuinely naive nature nor the achieved purity of
an artistic conscience. They are full of guilt and betrayal. Certainly
they do not belie the effervescent talent that he possessed, the impulse
and joy of the born storyteller. Just as in his social intercourse, there are
moments in Werfel's epical and dramatic works when he relaxed completely and gave himself up to his flowing gift, when he forgot and lost
himself, and therefore found himself, exposing the childlike basis of his
nature and its prankish exuberance. At such moments he told his story
well—impulsively, wittily, colorfully, even dramatically. On the whole,
however, he remained trapped between the spontaneity of the involun-
tary personal statement and the mental exertion of the work of art."[1]
    The poems however, Kahler concludes, occupy a special province
within the confines of this complex and self-contradictory personality:
they "reveal his inner history; that lovable childlike quality; that open-
ness to the world, that 'friendship with the world' which lay in the
depths of his nature, and the weakness, the abandonment to all tempta-
tions that are connected with these qualities; the urge toward union,
towards communication, towards mutual effect, and the inevitable
experience of the bounds separating person from person, of the impo-
tence of speech, of being alone with oneself."[2]
    But Franz Werfel's greatness lies precisely in the unbroken unity of
his statement. In his last collection of poems, on which he was working

[1] *Commentary*, V (1948), 186.
[2] *Ibid*, 187.

19

at the time of his death,[3] he included incredibly vulgar verses from his early work; while parts of his novels, the conversation with the bath-master in *Barbara*, Stephen's journey in *The Forty Days of Musa Dagh*, the "most important moment of his former life" in *Stern der Unge-borenen (Star of the Unborn)*, and nearly all of his short stories, par-ticularly "Das Trauerhaus" ("The House of Mourning"), have a ballad-like force and density that will preserve them from old age and death.

The phenomenal unevenness of quality evident in Werfel's work as a whole cannot be explained by the diversity of genres. It is more readily imputable to Werfel's nature, to an exuberant boyishness that sur-rendered itself wholly to every possible source of inspiration, and to his journalistic dependence on his subject matter. Werfel gave himself half as an enthusiast does to the thing he loves, half as a reporter to the thing he must deal with professionally. This twofold passivity on the part of his overflowing talent accounts for both the high and the low points in his work.

Was he, as Erich Kahler says, lacking in "that ultimate honor and honesty which are the premise of genuine artistic devotion?"[4] No, he possessed them to excess. He never dissembled, either in his person or in his works.

The comedian and journalist in him were authentic and superior. In his soul, playful improvisation dwelt side by side with the tragic and religious. Fear of the teacher dwelt close by the fear of God; and since they were combined in this very living and very creative man, it is not fitting to weigh, measure, and turn them against each other.

Franz Werfel was a good *and* a bad writer, a little boy *and* a whole man. He reported his life in these times as faithfully and as falsely as few writers have done. He was a mystical reporter, a traveler and explorer in that unknown country which he once called "inwardness" *(Innerlichkeit)*, and precisely because his report is so often distorted by the immediacy and formlessness of direct perception, it attests the exist-ence of an inner realm, the realm of the soul.

A volume of selections from early and for the most part forgotten or unpublished prose works by Werfel, edited and published by Adolf D. Klarmann as the first volume of his *Collected Works*, includes a sketch entitled "Cabrinowitsch." Cabrinowitsch was one of the assassins of the Austrian heir-apparent in Sarajevo; on his hands, he had the

[3] *Gedichte 1908-1945* (Poems 1908-1945), Los Angeles: Pazifische Presse, 1946.   [4] *Commentary, loc. cit.*, 187.

blood of the First World War. Werfel, a youth of twenty-five reluc-
tantly wearing uniform, saw the prisoner, tormented and sick to death,
before he was shipped off to his certain end in the dungeon of The-
resienstadt: "This face up in its cell, this kindness that has even ceased
to be painful, this oblique friendliness, this transfigured weakness—I
was shaken by the realization that this was the miraculously withdrawn
face of the very last of men, of him who is thrust from the midst, who
stands at the outermost edge of humanity. In these lost features, not
otherwise than in the face of a hero, I discerned the beauty and dignity,
the fatal, unthinkable loneliness of him who can never return to the
midst of men." and: ". . . All looked upon the shrunken aristocratic face
with the darkly tranquil eyes, there on the bier. And into their rough
souls the mystery penetrated. The men stood stiff at attention, embar-
rassed as though a superior were among them. A lamb had been
charged with the guilt. This being will receive nothing more, not even
a human death. And for that reason it towers over them all." ("Dies
Gesicht dort in der Zelle, diese nicht einmal mehr schmerzliche Güte,
diese schief geneigte Freundlichkeit, diese verklärte Schwäche, dies
wußte ich erschüttert, war das wundervolle entrückte Gesicht des
Allerletzten, dessen, der aus der Mitte gestoßen ist, der am äußersten
Rande der Menschheit steht. Nicht anders als auf dem Antlitz des
Helden erkannte ich in diesen verlorenen Zügen die Schönheit und
Würde der tödlichen unausdenklichen Einsamkeit dessen, der niemals
mehr in die Mitte der Menschen zurückkehren kann." und: ". . . Alle
blickten auf das kleingewordene adelige Gesicht mit den dunkel-
ruhigen Augen dort auf der Bahre. Und in die derben Seelen griff das
Geheimnis. Die Männer standen starr, habtacht, verlegen, als wäre ein
Vorgesetzter unter ihnen. Einem Lamm war die Schuld auferlegt
worden. Dieses Wesen wird nichts mehr empfangen, nicht einmal
einen Menschentod. Und darum übertrifft es alle.")[5]

Here we have the whole of Franz Werfel: the sharp realism, accompanied by the evil eye of the born epic poet; the courage, the foolhardy
courage of the ageless schoolboy, with which he plunged from reality
abruptly into the depths of the mystery; the immediate juxtaposition of
surface and inner meaning; the love and sympathy, the pathos; and
finally a stylistic bravura so great as to cast a doubt upon the authenticity of the vision. Ordinarily the seer pays with his blood for his

[5] *Erzählungen aus zwei Welten, I.* (Tales of Two Worlds), Stockholm: Bermann-
Fischer, 1948, 23, 26.

vision. But to Werfel visions were given in superfluity, as melodies were given to such composers as Mozart and Verdi. What was not given to Werfel was the strict measure of music; he did not mold what he saw; and the grace that befell him did not re-create him. He reported only what he observed, in a melody all his own that runs equally through his lyrical and his epic work.

Franz Kafka, with his innate sense of ultimate intellectual responsibility, noticed as early as 1912 this lack of artistic and human discipline. He called Werfel "a monster," and added: "But I looked him in the eye and held it all evening."[6] And about Werfel's poems he had said in the previous year that they filled his head like steam. "For a moment I feared the enthusiasm would carry me along straight into nonsense."[7]

Franz Werfel was a sublime reporter and he took over certain elements from the tradition of Austrian journalism whose last great representative, the satirist and pamphleteer Karl Kraus, was first his teacher and then his embittered enemy. It was from Austrian journalism that Werfel learned the art of the headline—the titles of his novels, as of each single one of his poems, are cabinet pieces of summation—it was here that he learned the sudden eruption of the narrative without preparation or exposition; the blurred ending, behind which stands the question mark of mystery, the mystery of a man or of all creation; the *bon mot*, through which, as through a crevice, one perceives the abyss; the strange fusing of psychology and musicality. But he also took over certain weaknesses of this essentially ephemeral genre: a certain flatness of perspective accompanied by a heavy laying on of color to stimulate depth; the point for the sake of the point; a tendency to heap up words; a weakness for digression, and long-windedness; the obtrusive "I." From the riches of the Austrian tradition and the abundance of his own imagination, he gathered at random; he did all he could do to keep pace with the flow of his own fancy; and so he had little time for structure and little energy for discipline. Even in his poems he was a reporter; but when in the course of a novel he paused and reflected, he became a great poet.

He was a reporter also in his highly developed flair for the "interesting" and his gift for presenting it. The story of the solemn vow with which Werfel introduced his *Song of Bernadette* is a case in point: After the collapse of France, in June 1940, he reached Lourdes in the

---

[6] *The Diaries of Franz Kafka 1910-1913,* New York: Schocken, 1948, 269.
[7] *Ibid.,* 189.

Pyrenees. There he acquainted himself with the miraculous story of Bernadette Soubirous. In his distress he pledged to "sing the Song of Bernadette" to the best of his possibilities and give this task priority over all other work, if only he was delivered from his predicament and allowed to reach the shores of America.[8] One does not even have to consider the propaganda use Hollywood made of this vow when the story was filmed—and considerably watered down—to agree with Erich Kahler when he says: "A pledge is a very serious private circumstance and anyone who took it as seriously as it deserved would feel some natural shyness about making it the sensational lead-horse of a new book."[9]

Nor did Franz Werfel, this most sociable of men, ever suffer from the loneliness and seclusion of the modern creative artist, of Proust or Joyce. There was always around him a banquet or an audience, whose applause he eagerly awaited. Franz Werfel was a festive, public phenomenon. Even when he was in exile and fatally ill, he collected people as a little boy collects butterflies. And this public, festive quality was another part of his Austrian heritage: Franz Werfel, the Prague Jew whom Hitler's laws drove half around the world, bore in the depth of his being the imprint of the baroque style that is preserved, gleaming and luxuriant, in the churches and palaces of his native land. Like baroque literature, his work made a public affair of faith, of the mystery of life and death, of ecstasy and repentance—did this by the seduction of words, the melody of language, by the modern dexterity with which he reported metaphysical problems and experience.

"It is fitting," Friedrich Torberg has said in a beautiful eulogy, "it is no accident and superficial whim that words like 'Song' and 'Aria' and 'Hymn' and 'Ballad' recur in the titles of his poems: 'Song of a Woman,' and 'Song of a Tramp,' a 'Drinking Song,' and a 'Spiritual Song,' a 'Death Song' and the 'Song of the World's Friend,' 'Dream Ballad' and 'Hymn of Tears' and 'Song After a Day Gone By.' Even one of his plays is called *Goat Song [Bocksgesang]* and even one of his novels, *The Song of Bernadette.* And it is fitting again that he could really sing and tear open his collar to be still better at it, and that he was able to look around, in his eyes the twinkle of an enthusiastic *gamin* and ask whether he should now impersonate the false falsetto of a German tenor or the mellifluous *shmalz* of an Italian one—and immediately afterwards he

[8] *The Song of Bernadette,* New York: Viking, 1942, 6, 7.
[9] *Commentary, loc. cit.,* 187.

was again completely carried away by music and melody. He sang because he had to sing, because he could not have endured not to sing —just as he could not endure to stay quietly in his seat at home when one of his beloved Verdi operas was broadcast. No, he was no listener, he did not remain passive, he performed and was a member of the cast, he jumped up and plunged into the scene and drew Rigoletto's dagger, emptied Alfredo's glass, and was the whole angry chorus of the priests as well as Rhadames, whom they condemned . . . ." (". . . Es paßt, es ist kein Zufall und keine Laune obenhin, daß in den Titeln seiner Gedichte 'Lied' und 'Gesang' und 'Hymnus' und 'Ballade' immer wiederkehren: 'Gesang einer Frau' und 'Gesang eines Lumpen,' ein 'Trinklied' und 'Ein geistliches Lied,' 'Todes-Gesang' und 'Der Weltfreund singt,' 'Traumballade' und 'Tränenhymnus' und 'Lied nach einem Tage,' und noch auf dem Theater konnte es 'Bocksgesang' heißen und noch im Roman 'Das Lied von Bernadette.' Und dazu fügt es sich abermals, daß er wirklich singen konnte und sich den Kragen aufreißen, um es noch besser zu können, und konnte plötzlich mit begeistertem Lausbuben—Blinzeln in die Runde fragen, ob er ihr nun lieber das Geknödel eines deutschen Tenors vorführen sollte oder Schmelz und Schmalz eines italienischen,—und gleich darauf war er schon wieder ganz dahingetragen von Musik und Melodie. Er sang, weil er singen mußte, weil er es nicht ertragen hätte, nicht zu singen—wie er es nicht ertrug, zuhause ruhig auf seinem Platz sitzen zu bleiben, wenn im Radio eine seiner geliebten Verdi-Opern übertragen wurde, nein, er war kein Zuhörer, er ließ sich nichts bieten, er wirkte mit, er sprang auf und mittenhinein und zog Rigolettos Dolch und leerte Alfredos Glas und war über Rhadames der ganze grollende Priesterchor . . . .")[10]

Often he was aware of the faultiness of his style. Then he attempted to lend significance to his own weakness by giving music the pre-eminence over language, by declaring the wordless to be the home and the salvation of his poor, weak word. "In einem Felsengrab, Das aus Musik gehauen ist, Möcht ich einst schlafen gehen," he writes in one of his later poems. ("Lay me to rest in a mountain grave carved out of music.")[11] And in a fragment of a novel, Black Mass (Die schwarze Messe), written in 1919, he wrote: "Is song not the most sacred symbol

[10] "Gedenkrede auf Franz Werfel" (Eulogy of Franz Werfel), Die Neue Rundschau (1946), 128, 129.

[11] "Das Felsengrab" (The Mountain Grave), Schlaf und Erwachen (Sleep and Awakening), Berlin: Zsolnay, 1935, 93.

of the lonely dialogue between God and man? The word bows down before music as a convict sentenced to life imprisonment bows down to a lonely ray of light in his cell at noon. The word is a poor sinner, confined to the prison of statement, but song, strong as a Samson, shatters the pillars of his house and raises the poor sinner aloft with unconquerable arms." ("Ist der Gesang nicht das heiligste Symbol der einsamen Zwiesprache zwischen Gott und Mensch?? Das Wort beugt sich vor dem Gesang wie ein lebenslänglich verurteilter Sträfling in seiner Zelle vor dem einzigen Sonnenstrahl zur Mittagsstunde. Das Wort ist ein armer Sünder, ins Zuchthaus seiner Aussage gesperrt, aber der Gesang, stark wie Simson, zerbricht die Säulen des Hauses und trägt mit unbesiegbaren Armen den armen Sünder empor.")[12]

Like all attempts at interpretation, this one has a certain apologetic quality and sidesteps the inner contradiction it set out to explain. With a style in which there is much local Prague jargon, much of the heritage of Viennese journalism, and a last gleam of the Hapsburg empire, of Maria Theresa no less than of Franz Joseph I, Franz Werfel was destined to plumb the depths of the modern soul.

Was he a Jew, a Catholic *extra muros,* a Russian Christian on the model of Dostoevsky? An answer would be meaningless. In a godless day, he presented local news of the kingdom of God. In this sense, his work is deserving of all honor.

[12] *Erzählungen,* 91.

WILMA BRUN MERLAN

Franz Werfel, Poet

Franz Werfel, a poet torn and divided between feeling and reason, is especially representative of his time in his emphasis on this division within man's nature. He begins to express this dividedness in his poetry and gives it more and more place in his prose plays, in his novels, and in his treatises concerning modern man's emphasis on the materialistic life and his neglect of the spiritual values.[1]

Werfel desires the spiritual life, although he is by nature a doubter—a highly intelligent product of our civilization, whose doubts make it impossible for him to live by faith, but whose desire for faith makes it impossible for him to accept the position of the agnostic.

In company with the expressionist poets of the period before and during World War I, Werfel is seeking for values that no longer exist or that do not yet exist. He deplores the fact that nations and individuals are judged by their power and by their material possessions and that these material goods are consequently desired. He regrets that in our highly mechanized world faith in the dignity of man and in the value of the human soul is disappearing. He points out the lack of affection among men. Along with others of his time, he calls attention to the dearth of human warmth in our civilization. He describes the individual seeking the companionship of his fellows over against an uncaring society. In these descriptions, however, a lack of harmony, reflected in the individual, becomes apparent. This individual is modern man—and he is Werfel himself.

The lack of harmony in Werfel's nature would seem to be the result of his living in a social environment with whose set of values or whose lack of values he is in disagreement; he expresses it (1) by dreaming

[1] Cf. especially *Spiegelmensch*, Kurt Wolff Vlg., München, 1920; *Realismus und Innerlichkeit* (Lecture), Paul Zsolnay Vlg., Berlin-Wien-Leipzig, 1931; *Barbara*, Paul Zsolnay Vlg., Wien, 1929; *Der veruntreute Himmel*, Bermann-Fischer Vlg., Stockholm, 1939.

of his childhood, (2) by wishing for friendships and relationships that do not exist, and (3) by describing his desire that men should overcome all human barriers and act as one manifestation of the same spirit. In his youthful poems of religious mysticism he looks forward to a life in which men will actually feel and act together. This belief is expressed again by the man of thirty-seven in "Dort und Hier" ("Here and There")[2]:

> Ja wir werden sein und uns erkennen,
> Nicht mehr machtlos zueinander brennen!
> . . . .
> Hier berühr ich dich. Dort wird's gelingen,
> Flamme, daß wir Flammen uns durchdringen;
> Und ich brenne tief, was wir hier litten,
> Dort im Geisterkuß dir abzubitten.

(Yes, there we will be and know each other, and no more burn powerlessly toward one another [as we do here]. Now I can only touch you. There, flame, we will succeed: As flames we shall penetrate each other. And I shall burn deeply to ask your forgiveness, in a spirit kiss, for what we suffered here.)[3]

Poems such as the above show that the Werfel who wants to live in harmony with his social, material, and political environment yet seeks a solution quite independent of this world around him.

✿   ✿   ✿   ✿   ✿   ✿

Werfel's first volume of poetry, *Der Weltfreund* (1908-10) reveals his desire to be one with all men, to love and be loved by them, his dissatisfaction with a lonely present and a consequent desire for the far-off, happy time of childhood when inanimate things—his toys, his books, his bed—seemed to have a soul and to recognize him as their friend. He longs for play with his little sister and for the love of mother and nurse. In "Gottvater am Abend" ("God the Father in the Evening"), God himself longs for the warmth of human contact and laments that as the creator of all he has no one to pray to, no one to tend to his needs:

> Ich bin nie durch Zimmer gesprungen,
> Trieb niemals am Spielplatz herum,
> Und meine Erinnerungen
> Sind ewig und alt und stumm.

---

[2] *Gedichte*, Paul Zsolnay Vlg., Berlin-Wien-Leipzig, 1927, p. 430.
[3] In translating the quoted poems, the writer has not made any attempt to keep

> Bin niemals hinausgetreten
> In Schicksals empfangenden Pfad,
> Zu wem soll ich einziger beten?
> Umringt von tausend Planeten
> Weiß ich mir keinen Rat.
>
> Nun sind die Lichtlein vergangen,
> Nun schlaft ihr auf Erden geschart,
> Nun wein ich in meinen langen,
> Langen weißen Bart.[4]

(Never have I skipped through rooms, never have I drifted about playgrounds, and my memories are eternal and old and without sound. Never have I stepped forth to interfere with fate [in fate's receiving path]. To whom shall I, the unique and only one, pray? Ringed about by a thousand planets, I know of no advice [or counsel] for myself. Now the small lights [of earth] are gone, now you are grouped in sleep upon the earth; now I weep into my long, long, white beard.)

Compared with God's apartness, man's life, especially his childhood, has many satisfying associations. It is with lingering regret that Werfel leaves these childhood pleasures and attempts to enlarge the circle by turning toward men. He asks for their friendship and understanding. He expresses himself very shyly, but all the more intensely, because he has very early become aware that his calling as a poet will set him apart from other men. He wants to feel that he can be of use to them:

> Wärst du bedürftig doch,
> Daß ich dir helfen könnt!
> Wärst du krank doch,
> Daß ich dich trösten könnt!
> Wärst du müde doch
> Daß ich dich betten könnt!
> Du braver Mensch!
> . . . .
> . . . .
> Komm! verschmähe mich nicht!
> Freundschaft biet ich dir an
> Du braver Mensch![5]

(Oh that you were needy, that then I might help you! Oh that you were ill,

---

the original rhythm. In some of the poems the translation is quite literal, in others it is free; sometimes a word or words are added in order to clarify the meaning, or an alternate translation is given in brackets.

[4] *Der Weltfreund*, Kurt Wolff Vlg., München, 1920, p. 43.   [5] *Ibid.*, p. 102.

that then I might comfort you! Oh that you were tired that I might cradle
you! You honorable and upright human . . . you man! . . . Come! Do not
disdain me! Friendship I offer you, you honorable man!)

At the same time he stresses the difference between himself, the poet,
and other men. Life pours through him as through a transparent vessel,
while other men are impenetrable, like iron and wood:

> Ja, nur ich bin wie Glas,
> Durch mich schleudert die Welt ihr schäumendes Übermaß.
> Die andern sind, wie Eisen und Holz,
> Auf ihren festen Charakter, die Undurchstrahlbarkeit stolz.
> Manchmal schaun sie zu mir hin,
> Und sehn mich nur, wenn ich vom durchdringenden Strom blind
> und qualmig bin.[6]

(Yes, only I, only I am as glass, through me the world hurls its foaming
excess. Others are, as iron and wood, proud of their firm character, their
impenetrability. Sometimes, those others, they look at me and see me only
when I am opaque and cloudy from the stream that is pouring through me.)

However, the poet forgets his apartness long enough to express his
delight in just being in and of the world:

> Ich will mich auf den Rasen niedersetzen,
> Und mit der Erde in den Abend fahren.
> O Erde, Abend, Glück, O auf der Welt sein!![7]

(On earth's grass will I sit down and with the earth travel into the next
sunset. O earth, O evening, O happiness, O-being-in-the-world!!)

Werfel has a philosophy that all men and all things are manifestations
of the same spirit. A knowledge of this spiritual relationship should
cause men to love one another and to love all of creation, animate or
inanimate, with which they come in contact. "Die vielen Dinge" ("The
Many Things") merely hints at such a philosophy, which will be repeated frequently in his later poems:

> . . . .
> Du bist es selbst, was nimmer du besitzt,
> Und nennst es: Wein, Greis, Mitzi, Rosen!
> . . . .
> Bist eins mit ihm und wirst es nie verstehn,

[6] *Ibid.,* p. 91.
[7] *Ibid.,* p. 88.

> Du liebst, und liebst dich selbst als Irgendwen.
> O du Gestalt des ewig Wesenlosen![8]

(You are yourself that thing which you never possess, and you name it: wine, old man, Mitzi, roses. You are one with it, and yet will never understand it. You love, loving, and love yourself while you love anybody (or anything). You are yourself the form of the eternally formless.)

The author believes that our individual forms are a hindrance to our fullest development:

> Eine Wandlung trennt nich vom Höchsten nur:
> Noch bin ich Wesen,
> Noch bin ich Person![9]

(One metamorphosis, [one changing-over], still separates me from the Highest: Yet am I Being, Yet am I Person.)

The keynote of *Der Weltfreund* is not one of discouragement, however. The poet believes that to some extent we can break down the barriers between ourselves and others by doing good deeds:

> Herz frohlocke!
> Eine gute Tat habe ich getan.
> Nun bin ich nicht mehr einsam.
> Ein Mensch lebt,
> Es lebt ein Mensch,
> Dem die Augen sich feuchten,
> Denkt er an mich.[10]

(Heart rejoice! I have done a good deed. Now I am no longer lonely. A man lives, there lives a fellow-mortal whose eyes moisten when he thinks of me.)

This is Werfel, the expressionist, for whom the world has its beginning in, and receives its meaning from, man. Very strongly he states this longing for human relationships in the poem "An den Leser" ("To the Reader"):

> Mein einziger Wunsch ist, Dir, O Mensch verwandt zu sein!
> Bist du Neger, Akrobat, oder ruhst du noch in tiefer Mutterhut,
> Klingt dein Mädchenlied über den Hof, lenkst Du dein Floß
>   im Abendschein,
> Bist Du Soldat, oder Aviatiker voll Ausdauer und Mut.
>   . . . .

[8] *Ibid.*, p. 57.   [9] *Ibid.*, p. 82.   [10] *Ibid.*, p. 104.

So gehöre ich Dir und allen!
Wolle mir bitte nicht widerstehn!
O, könnte es einmal geschehn,
Daß wir uns, Bruder, in die Arme fallen.[11]

(My only wish is, fellow-mortal, to be related to you! Whether you be
Negro, acrobat, or whether you are still resting deep in the mother's womb,
whether your girlish song sounds across the yard, or whether you guide
your raft in the evening sun, whether you be soldier or aviator full of per-
severance and courage . . . . So I belong to you and to all! Do not, please,
resist me, O would that some time, some place . . . brother, we might
embrace.)

✼   ✼   ✼   ✼   ✼   ✼

In *Der Weltfreund* Werfel has hinted that, within their physical existence, all men are spiritually related. He develops this idea in *Wir sind*
(1911-12). Here, in addition, the dividedness hinted at in *Der Weltfreund* becomes more apparent. But the prevailing mood is still a hopeful one, however, because men are in the world, and are in the world
together:

Wer handelnd sich empörte
Bedenke doch! Unsagbar
Mit Reden und Gestalten
Sind wir uns fern und nah!
Daß wir hier stehn und sitzen
Wer kann's beklommen fassen?!
Doch über allen Worten
Verkünd 'ich Mensch, *Wir sind.*[12]

(Whoever has, in living, rebelled against life, let him consider! Beyond our
speaking and being, yet are we intermingled, each in the other. Who, aston-
ished, can grasp the simple fact of our sitting and standing here? For beyond and above all words: I tell you, mortal man, *we are!*)

In the concluding remarks to *Wir sind*[13] Werfel makes the statement
that he believes it possible for all that is humanly dignified, for goodness, happiness, joy, sorrow, loneliness, and for ideals to arise out of this
eternal, impenetrable, powerful *Existenzbewußtsein* (consciousness
of existence) that he calls *Frömmigkeit* (piety).

Continued from *Der Weltfreund,* there is a note of pessimism due to

[11] *Ibid.,* p. 109f.
[12] *Wir sind,* Kurt Wolff Vlg., Leipzig, 1914, p. 76.
[13] *Ibid.,* Nachwort, p. 125.

the belief that man's human form puts a barrier between him and
others. This makes it impossible for human beings actually to understand and "have" each other in spite of being manifestations of one spirit:

> Wir drehen uns vorüber
> An einem Lämpchen, einem Mann.
> Uns reißt etwas hinüber,
> Und letzte Sehnsucht faßt uns an.
> Wir werden nie uns haben,
> Denn Formsein packt uns herrisch ein.
> Und sind wir einst begraben,
> Wird Staub dem Staub noch feindlich sein.[14]

(We can only whirl past each other, past a light post, past a man. Something draws us almost together, but even as this final longing seizes us, we
can never have each other. For this existence within a form encloses us
straitly and keeps us apart. And even within the tomb, dust will still be
hostile to dust.)

The last stanza of this poem reveals that the poet is not left without
hope:

> Verheißung letzter Treue
> Ist unserer Augen Bruderlicht,
> Aus dem die Winterbläue
> Der ungedämmten Himmel bricht.
> Daß wir dereinst uns finden
> In den Gefühlen ohne Sprung,
> Durch uns, in uns verschwinden,
> Und Schwung sind, nichts als Schwung, und Lieb'
> und jagende Begeisterung.[15]

(The brotherly light of our eyes is the prophecy of final future loyalty, and
out of our eyes shines forth the winter-blue of heavens unrestrained. Some
day we shall find each other, fused in our feelings. We shall disappear
through and within each other and become pure flight together, nothing
but flight and love and the forward rush of our twined spirits.)

The volume ends on this note of desire to overcome all human
barriers by means of love. Indeed, it says that we are merely children
until we have been able to lose our identity in every living thing,
until we have suffered the pain and sorrow of the meanest creature,
that is, until we have attained complete understanding:

[14] *Ibid.*, p. 80.   [15] *Ibid.*, p. 80.

O Herr, zerreiße mich!

. . . .

Begnade mich mit Martern, Stich um Stich!
Ich will den Tod der ganzen Welt einschließen.
O Herr, zerreiße mich![16]

(O Lord, tear me apart! . . . Bless me with torments, thrust for thrust. I would embrace the death of all the world. O Lord, dismember me!)

✿ ✿ ✿ ✿ ✿ ✿

Werfel has said in his first two volumes of poetry that the world begins with man, but he becomes more and more aware of the gulf between what man is and what he ought to be. *Einander* (1913-14) does not deny the *Lebensbejahung* (affirmation of life) of *Wir sind,* but it says that this will be possible only when man has become united with his fellow-men in brotherly love:

Komm heiliger Geist du, schöpferisch!
Den Marmor unsrer Form zerbrich!
Daß nicht mehr Mauer krank und Hart
Den Brunnen dieser Welt umstarrt,
Daß wir gemeinsam und nach oben
Wie Flammen in einander toben![17]

(Come holy spirit, creator, destroy the rigid marble of our form, so that no longer may this sick, hard wall stiffly surround the fountain of this world, that we, together, and all reaching upward, shall rage together upward, like a flame of joined flames.)

The mood of the book is one of tender melancholy, with an occasional expression of hope.

✿ ✿ ✿ ✿ ✿ ✿

In *Der Gerichstag (The Day of Judgment,* 1916-17), written in the trenches, the author fights an agonizing and almost hopeless battle with despair and heartbreak. To be sure, the spiritual relationship of men is cause for rejoicing, but they have forgotten their divine origin and this is the cause of their lovelessness. Only a miracle can save them, and Werfel prays that the miracle may happen.

The poet has begun to doubt if there is a means to bridge the gulf between individuals. Words cannot do it; in fact, they often do the op-

[16] *Ibid.,* p. 92.
[17] *Einander,* Kurt Wolff Vlg., München, 1920, p. 29.

posite. Werfel envies those creatures who *are* and do not need to *say*.
He laments his having been created for idle words rather than for deeds.
He says to the lark with envying admiration: "Du tust dein Leben, du
schwebst deinen Sang, und du bist was du bist."[18] ("You *do* your life,
you 'fly' your song, and you are what you are.") He is convinced that
the poet's medium is utterly inadequate:

> Ach, es ist nicht gut zu sagen,
> Denn wer sagt, versagt.[19]

(Oh, it is not good to say, for he who speaks fails to convey meaning [for
he who says, non-says].)

In a very strange poem[20] Werfel questions whether there is anything
except words and begins to doubt God's plan of redemption. If the dog
barks in order to give expression to its wishes, and if man uses the word
for the same purpose, then are not all of us—men, stars, and the whole
of creation—only sounds expressing God's desires? If this is the case,
everything is only word (rather than deed), and therefore death reigns.

Most of the poems in this volume express Werfel's recognition of the
misery of man, caused by lovelessness. He says that God will judge not
those who have loved, but only the lukewarm and the divided per-
sonalities. From the later group he does not exclude himself:

> Warum hast du mich mit diesem Feind erschaffen, mein Vater,
> . . . .
> Warum gabst du mir nicht Einheit und Reinheit?
> Reinige, einige mich, oh du Gewässer![21]

(Why have you created me with this inner enemy, my Father, why did
you not give me unity and purity? Purify, unify me, O you Father of
Waters.)

The double nature in man has led the poet to assume a dividedness
in God. He speaks of the world as the night upon God's face, of man's
breathing as the throbbing of God's wound. Because of his double
nature God is not yet complete. The task which Werfel sees for the
individual is not only that of redeeming and perfecting his fellow-man,
but also of helping God to realize himself. He sees in every new-born
child a possible redeemer:

[18] *Der Gerichtstag*, Kurt Wolff Vlg., Leipzig, 1919, p. 35.   [19] *Ibid.*, p. 87.
[20] From *Beschwörungen* in *Gedichte*, 1927, p. 368f.
[21] *Der Gerichtstag*, p. 250.

> Noch im schlammigsten Antlitz
> Harret das Gott-Licht seiner Entfaltung.
> Die gierigen Herzen greifen nach Kot,—
> Aber in jedem
> Geborenen Menschen
> Ist mir die Heimkunft des Heilands verheißen.[22]

(Even in the slimiest face the God-light is awaiting its development. Even while the greedy hearts of men reach out toward the mire—I see in every man born the arrival of the savior.)

The poet encourages man to do holy deeds and in this way to help God in his realization:

> Komm, komm, Mensch! Nur du wirst durch heilige Taten
> Die werdende Gottheit lassen geraten.
> Aus dieser Wirrsal, dem Wahn und dem Scheinen
> Wirst du die Vielfalt zur Einfalt vereinen.[23]

(Come, come and try man! Only you, man, through your holy deeds, can create the Godhead. Out of confusion, madness, and semblance, Man will unite diversity into Unity [of God].)

*   *   *   *   *   *

Der Gerichtstag is the last collection of poems to show some originality of thought. In *Schlaf und Erwachen*[24] and in *Gedichte*[25] the poet continues to ask God to destroy the enemy within him that causes him to act "dividedly." He asks to be God's voice when he speaks and God's pen when he writes. In the prose epilogue to *Gedichte*[26] the author says that he has not changed his truest and most essential judgments. The early poems that he chose for inclusion in this 1927 volume still represent the feeling of the older Werfel. The poems of his middle age do not tell us anything essential about the poet. In *Beschwörungen (Incantations, 1918-22)*[27], in *Schlaf und Erwachen,*[28] and in his 1938 and 1943[29] collections he writes sensitively about his approaching old age, about illness, about death, about the suffering of the Jewish population

[22] *Ibid.,* p. 151.   [23] *Ibid.,* p. 230.
[24] *Schlaf und Erwachen,* Paul Zsolnay Vlg., Berlin-Wien-Leipzig, 1935.
[25] *Gedichte,* 1927.
[26] *Ibid.,* p. 446.
[27] From *Beschwörungen* in *Gedichte,* 1927.
[28] *Gedichte aus den Jahren, 1908-1945,* Bermann-Fischer Vlg., Stockholm, 1946.
[29] *Ibid.*

of Vienna under National Socialist domination; but in these poems he is no longer able to combat his world-weariness and his resignation. There is nothing here to set him apart from any other sensitive writer.

The poems that have real literary and human value come from the young Franz Werfel, the poet of Expressionism.

❋   ❋   ❋   ❋   ❋   ❋

Some knowledge of Werfel's style is essential to an understanding of his poems. He belonged to the expressionist school, a school that attempted to give the word new power by stripping it of associations, and doing away with all nonessentials. Edschmid says:

> Auch das Wort erhält andere Gewalt—Es wird Pfeil. Trifft . . .
> in das Innere des Gegenstands und wird von ihm beseelt. Es
> wird kristallisch das eigentliche Bild des Dinges.[30]

(The word receives new power . . . it becomes an arrow. It strikes the heart of the object, and is animated by the object. The word becomes, crystal-like, the actual picture of the object.)

The verb has new powers of expression; articles and attributive words are discarded by many expressionist poets; some speak only in cries and outbursts. Werfel does not go to extremes in his use of language, as do some of the expressionists;[31] he does, however, do away with the article at times; words receive new meanings *(Versagen = falsch sagen;* to fail, to be found wanting = to say falsely); prefix and verb are usually one word in independent clauses: ("In Duft und Ruhe niederfällt dein Haar!!") ("In fragrance and quiet downfalls your hair!!")[32] He often makes use of abstractions for carrying the idea:

> Es ist kein Sinn
> In dem Ichbin!
> . . . .
>
> Ichbin ist um mich. Ich bin eingeschlossen
> Und Unentrinnbar ist der zweite Name der Welt![33]

[30] Kasimir Edschmid, *Über den Expressionismus in der Literatur und die Neue Dichtung,* Reisz Vlg., Berlin, 1921, p. 66.

[31] *Menschheitsdämmerung,* Ernst Rowohlt Vlg., Berlin, 1922. Cf. poems of August Stramm, pp. 24 and 36; Albert Ehrenstein, p. 45f; Walter Hasenclever, p. 89; Gottfried Benn, p. 88; Johannes R. Becher, p. 110; Ernst Stadler, p. 129.

[32] *Beschwörungen* in *Gedichte,* Paul Zsolnay Vlg., Berlin-Wien-Leipzig, 1927, p. 338.

[33] *Einander,* Kurt Wolff Vlg., München, 1920, p. 35.

(There is no meaning in the I-am. 'I-am' is round about me! I am locked in on myself. 'Inescapable' is the second name for the world.)

It is particularly in *Gerichtstag* that he indulges too often in abstractions, and consequently the pictures lose in clarity and reality. To some extent he overcomes the difficulty by using parables.[34]

The frequent use of dialogue and stichomythea reveals the author's own lack of harmony. The poem "Sarastro" shows him both as the doubter and as the believer:

> Adept: Wie ferne noch das Gottesreich auf Erden?
> Sarastro: Von dir durch Aug und Mund kann es begonnen werden.
> Adept: Bin ich nicht einer, der des Heiles harrt?
> Sarastro: Der Heiland kommt nicht. Er ist Gegenwart.
> Adept: Wie soll ich seine Gegenwart beginnen?
> Sarastro: Sei tausend Außen, und sei Eins nach innen! . . .[35]

(Adept: How far away, still, is God's kingdom on earth?
Sarastro: It can be begun by you through eye and mouth [by look and speech].
Adept: Am I not as one awaiting salvation?
Sarastro: The savior is not coming. He is the present.
Adept: How shall I begin His presence?
Sarastro: Be a thousand outward beings, and one united being within yourself! . . .)

When the poet is expressing genuine feeling, his poetry is usually simple and beautiful; when he begins to preach or attempts to force goodness in himself and others, his language becomes forced. To this tortured sentence structure correspond tortured pictures—pictures of disease, decay, wounds, horror, and death. Sometimes horror and gruesomeness are found together in one poem with tenderness and beauty as in "Jesus und der Äser-Weg" ("Jesus and the Carrion-Path").[36] This poem describes Jesus' prayer to the father to help him overcome his aversion toward any part of nature and to help him love the decaying and repulsive dead animal bodies floating past in a stream, and God's granting of this prayer. The poem then describes Jesus bedecking his hair, shoulders, and girdle with small animal corpses and the resultant rejoicing of nature and the appearance of the dove of God in the sun-filled air.

[34] Cf. "Verwundeter Storch" in *Gerichtstag*, p. 74.
[35] *Einander*, p. 94.
[36] From *Einander* in *Gedichte*, 1927, p. 218ff.

❈   ❈   ❈   ❈   ❈   ❈

Werfel's poems bring out the following aspects of his nature: (1) reason as against feeling; (2) preaching as against exemplary living (or being); (3) the individual as against the world; (4) the individual (and the world) as against God, and the reverse—God as against the individual and the world. In Werfel's youthful poems feeling predominates, whereas he becomes more and more the preacher and the poet of reason as he grows older and as he experiences the horror in the world about him.

When he emphasizes the polarity that exists between the individual and the world, it is always the spiritual man that he has in mind over against a materialistic world, a world which has forgotten its divine origin and has fallen away from God. This spiritual man is Werfel's ideal. But, as was emphasized in *Der Gerichtstag*, even the most spiritual man is God's opposite; he is that part of God which is divided against itself. God is aware of this polarity and is awaiting his redemption through man. And so Werfel's highest wish for mankind is the continued redemption of man through God and through his fellow-man. It is this redeemed man who can, in turn, redeem God himself:

> Kind, wie ich dich mit meinem Blut erlöste,
> So wart ich weinend, daß du mich erlöst.[37]

(Child, just as I redeemed you with my blood, so do I, weeping, wait for you to redeem me.)

[37]From *Einander* in *Gedichte*, 1920, p. 224.

FRANK WOOD

The Role of "Wortschuld" in Werfel's Poetry

In a recent essay on Werfel a German critic has stated: "Although he was fond of life, he lived in our godless age with the feeling of such frightful and unimaginable alienation, only comparable perhaps to Hoelderlin's alienation from his own age, a poet with whom Werfel otherwise has very little in common."[1] It might be worth-while to examine further into this condition of spiritual alienation in a world where the *deus absconditus* is so signally prominent and, more specifically, into an artistic dilemma reflected in the work of both Hoelderlin and Werfel, though under quite different auspices.

In Hoelderlin's *Empedokles* (first version) there is the following well-known passage:

> EMPEDOKLES— . . . . Die Götter waren
> Mir dienstbar nun geworden, ich allein
> War Gott und sprachs im frechen Stolz heraus.
> O glaub es mir, ich wäre lieber nicht
> Geboren.
>
> (EMPEDOKLES— . . . . The gods
> Stood now in service to me, I alone
> Was god and uttered it in insolent pride.
> O believe my word, rather that I had not
> Been born.)

To which his disciple Pausanias replies:

> Was? Um eines Wortes willen?
> Wie kannst du so verzagen, kühner Mann?
>
> (What? For the sake of a mere word?
> How can you so lose courage, dauntless man?)

[1] Paul Stöcklein, "Franz Werfel," in *Deutsche Literatur im 20. Jahrhundert*, hrsg. von Hermann Friedman und Otto Mann, Heidelberg, 1954, p. 282.

39

Empedokles' response is emphatic:

> Um eines Wortes willen. Ja.
>
> (For the sake of a word. Yes.)

Empedokles' guilt, as Benno von Wiese has pointed out, was not his claim to be divine but that he lent expression to this claim, a kind of "Wortschuld" (word-guilt) "bei der das falsche Nennen und Mitteilen bereits Schuld bedeutet." ("where wrong communication and use of words already signifies guilt.")[2]

The evolution of Werfel's poetic language is very interesting in itself, especially since his utterances on this point display a singular awareness, not to say self-consciousness. That in his growth as a poet he was quite early confronted with the tragic implications of a "Wortschuld" is clearly indicated in his early lyrics, especially in the collection *Der Gerichtstag* (1916-17), containing over forty passages dealing with the vulnerable status of the poetic word. Just what the nature of this "Wortschuld" is and how it differs from that of Hoelderlin's *Empedokles* are questions that reflect back on a century of development in the German lyric and to which we shall return later.

Already in *Der Weltfreund* (1908-10) Werfel was concerned with the quality of his poetic medium, still echoing Rilke, however, and others similarly pressed by the necessity of a new symbolic language:

> Ihr armen Worte, abgeschabt und glatt,
> Die Sprache und die Mode hat euch satt,
> Von zuviel Ausgesprochensein verheert
> Seid ihr schon schal und doch wie sehr bedauernswert . . .
>
> (You poor words, smooth and worn away,
> Fashion and language had their fill of you,
> And ravaged now through so much utterance
> And so insipid, yet how pitiable . . .)

In other poems, like "Der Dichter" ("The Poet"), the transparency of the true poet, a pane of glass reflecting true experience, is established in ironical inversion: the Others, the non-poets, proud of their opacity, take notice of the poet only when his mirror, like theirs, is clouded with

[2] Benno von Wiese, *Die Deutsche Tragödie von Lessing bis Hebbel*, München, 1935, p. 356; also Paul Böckmann, *Hoelderlin und seine Götter*, München, 1935, p. 188 *passim*.

foreign matter. There is, in fact, hardly a volume of the early Werfel's verse which does not contain a number of poems dealing with the treachery of the poetic word in its modern setting. In the *Nachwort* to the collection of *Wir sind* (1913), for instance, the thought of the previous poem is given greater expansion in prose. The poet, writes Werfel, knows that he is closest to life even in his "shoreless exaltations" and "controllable madnesses" *(kontrollierbare Wahnsinne)*. His value as artist is not determined by himself but by the necessity of the work he is engaged in. So indispensable is the poetic product that the world would have ceased to exist if it were not there. Finally, the poet knows of a certainty that this necessary work *(das Notwendige seines Lebens)*, though it be sullied by all the waters of vanity and commonness, is nevertheless God-willed *(Gottgewollt)*. In the light of Werfel's first humanitarian outcry "Mein einziger Wunsch ist dir, O Mensch, verwandt zu sein" ("O Man, my only wish is to be related to you"), there is enormous irony in the insight divulged by Memnon's column in the poem by that name ("Gesang der Memnonssäule"): "Unmenschlich ist/Der Menschliche, der Dichter." ("Inhuman is/the human, the poet.")

The problem confronting Werfel had already been formulated by Hofmannsthal's Lord Chandos (1901), to go no further back, and at mid-century it is still the concern, perhaps more urgent than ever before, of writers like Heinrich Böll and Albert Camus. Lord Chandos had discovered, as a result of his penetration of experience, that it was impossible for him to continue to write in any known tongue except it were "a language, none of whose words are familiar, a language in which mute things speak to me . . . ."[3] Reduced to its simplest form, it is the problem arising from the conflict between language and conscience within the artist himself.

The precariousness of the situation is frequently revealed in Werfel's poetry by the almost synonymous connotation of terms like "Wort" (word), "Spiegel" (mirror), and "Lüge" (lie). Unlike Shelley's skylark ("An eine Lerche"), whose life is its song, the modern poet is caught in the division between the two; existentially he is not what he *is:*

> Oh du Leben, einfältiger Punkt,
> Du bist nicht unser!

[3] Hugo von Hofmannsthal, "Ein Brief," *Gesammelte Werke, Prosa II,* Frankfurt a.M., 1951, p. 22 ". . . eine Sprache, von deren Worten mir auch nicht eines bekannt ist, eine Sprache, in welcher die stummen Dinge zu mir sprechen . . . ."

> Denn wir lügen,
> Wir brüllen und stieren,
> Stößt uns der Wächter zur Suppe.
> Viel fürchten wir
> Unsern Herrscher, den Hieb.—
> Und so nicht sind wir, was wir sind.
>
> (Oh vital bird, simplicity's center,
> You're no kin of ours.
> For we lie
> And we bellow with vacant stare
> When the overseer pushes us to the meal-trough.
> And much do we fear
> Our lord and master, the lash.—
> And thus we are never what we are.)

The poetic word, again, runs the risk of issuing too soon in finality, the prematurely closed horizon (and Werfel himself was often vulnerable in this respect): "Ein rundes Wort, ein runder Laut, der endet und schließt . . . ." (A rounded word, a rounded sound that ends and closes . . . .") Hoelderlin's Empedokles could have spoken the following lines:

> Ach, es ist nicht gut zu sagen,
> Denn wer sagt, versagt . . .
>
> (Alas, it is harmful to speak,
> For who speaks, mis-speaks . . .)

Rilke would have responded fully to the following:

> Viele Worte sind uns gegeben.
> Es schielt unser Leben mit Worten,
> Die wir befehden . . .
>
> (Many words are given to us,
> And our life is squinty with words
> Which we embroil . . .)

The shade of Nietzsche, one of the prime forerunners of Expressionism, frowns from the following lines:

> Du traue nicht den Männern des zweiten Worts.
> Den Wider-Wörtlern, den Antwörtlern.
>
> (And you, do not trust the men of the second word,
> Who counter with words and answer with words.)

As antidote to such verbal corruption Werfel simply proposes "die Stummheit Gottes" and his silence:

> Oh leise! Kein Ausbruch jetzt! Bebt! Schweigt!
> Oh Schwestern; du Volk, es ist wahr, ja es ist wahr.
> Weint nicht kurz hin, ihr Lieben!
> Haltet fest in eurer Kehle den Gott!
>
> (O softly! No outburst now! Tremble. Be still!
> O Sisters, my people, it is true, true, indeed.
> Yield not to brief weeping, you loved ones!
> Let not the god escape from your throats!)

Nowhere is the difference between the two kinds of word—the banal communication of everyday speech and the truly poetic idiom born of inner communion with experience—more clearly (and grotesquely) articulated than in the poem "Unmut" ("Ill Humor"). On the one hand, there is the prefabricated language of every day, a mere sign language; on the other, the true poetic medium which groans in captivity for its essential freedom—"gebunden, angekettet, gesetzt" ("bound, chained, harmless"). The *mise en scène* of the poem is that of a prison where false words act as wardens and police spies in typically bourgeois roles, while the poet,

> Der Sträfling,
> Nagt an der Luke, nagt an dem Eisen-Gitter,
> Und kann nicht entwischen.
>
> (The convict
> Gnaws at the narrow window, the iron grill,
> And cannot escape.)

The irony is that the imprisoned poet is, after all, "der erhabene Ausreißer" ("the majestic runaway") compared with his jailors who are "starr, pünktlich, hornhäutige Bauern" ("cold, punctual, callous farmers"). In short, some of Werfel's most bitter baroque epithets are reserved for this deterioration of the poetic word from its high function as a citadel of truth, e.g. "die langwortigen Würmer" ("long-wordy worms"), "lange Streifen von Worten" ("long strips of words"), "an einem Lügenzunder Worts" ("on a tinder of word-lies"), "meines Lügens Lügenwiderhall" ("the lie-echo of my lying"), etc. At the same time we are granted a glimpse of what the real, the true word might be, the word singular instead of plural, later to be visualized as the

44 F R A N Z   W E R F E L

eternal Alpha and Omega: "Jetzt treiben wir noch Worte,/Einst haben
wir nur Wort." ("We still make a business of *words*/Some day we shall
possess only *word.*") For the poet at this stage the health-bringing word
is "surrender" *(Hingabe)*, just as later, for Werfel, the state of poetic
concentration or self-collectedness *(Sammlung)* will depend upon grace
and not upon self-will. Indeed, in the collection of poems called *Beschwörungen* the arrow is already pointing in that direction:

> Was mir gelingt,
> Darf nicht mir gelingen.
> Ein andres Wesen will aus mir dringen,
> Während mein Wachsein sinkt . . .
>
> (What is my success
> Is not due to me.
> Another being seeks to issue from me
> As consciousness ebbs away . . .)

The poet is likened to the eternal St. Sebastian with all the world's
arrows in his breast, surrounded by the entire creation (more than
mere world) awaiting his redeeming word.

If, then, the poet is the "name-giver" and his poem the necessary
creation, without which the world would have ceased to exist, his
ethical responsibility is indeed very great. How wholeheartedly Werfel
must have endorsed the tenor of Thomas Mann's letter to the dean of
Bonn University when it deprived him of his honorary doctorate: "The
mystery of language is a great one; the responsibility for a language
and its purity is of a symbolic and spiritual kind; this responsibility
does not have merely an aesthetic sense. The responsibility for language
is, in essence, human responsibility . . . ."[4]

The dilemma of language presented a conflict in which Werfel's
entire generation was deeply involved, whether we call the two oppos-
ing forces literary structure, on the one hand, and ethical involvement
on the other; or simply Expressionism as a style and Expressionism as a
movement. "Peculiar to our poetic youth today which feels so abandoned," Franz Blei was writing in 1917, "is the almost indignant feeling
of shame which it feels when it has succeeded in creating a beautiful
poem. This feeling is frequently so strong that young poets would
preferably indulge in the poem that is 'ugly,' or merely 'shout' their

[4] "The Hollow Miracle—Notes on the German Language," trans. George Steiner,
The Reporter, XXII (Feb. 18, 1960), p. 39.

despair of humanity in view of the lack of moral standards in the world. The conscience of our young is weighted down by the question whether it were not better to accomplish a work of merely moral rather than of aesthetic value. This attitude gives voice, among other things, to despair resulting from the lack of a form-creating society .... This the poet himself cannot create, for since his whole activity is inter-sharing *(Mit-Teilung),* the existence of the other factor, the form-creating milieu, must be presupposed if this is to come to pass, and such a milieu is lacking."[5] A similar note of indignant shame and despair, sometimes blended with romantic irony and self-parody, is often heard in Werfel's early work:

> Hinter jedem Wort stockt Scham. . .
> Was haben wir, da wir sagten, getan . . .
> Die Welt ist uns von Wortes Art,
> Als Lüge weh auf halbem Weg erstarrt.
>
> (Behind each word lurks shame . . .
> What crime did we do when we spoke? . . .
> For us the world is a pattern of words,
> A wounded lie stiff on the road half done.)

And as for the form-creating society which is prerequisite to the poet's proper functioning:

> So blieb uns nur
> Des Jahrmarkts Spiegellabyrinth . . .
>
> (So for us is left only
> The mirror-labyrinth of the county fair . . .)

To come back to Hoelderlin again, the problem of the "Wortschuld" as treated in *Empedokles* is of a somewhat different nature than Werfel's own problem, nor could it hardly be otherwise. To be sure, Empedokles-Hoelderlin is likewise aware of guilt in the use of the word, but its origin is located elsewhere. Language is limited, according to Hoelderlin, to the peculiarly human sphere in the narrower sense and fails when confronted with those marginal areas in which the greater life-powers *(Lebensmächte)* become operative. When Hyperion, for example, says of his conversations with Diotima that they spoke very little and were ashamed of their language when all one wanted was to become a tone and to fuse in one divine song *(Himmelsgesang),*

[5] Franz Blei, quoted in *Ahnung und Aufbruch: Expressionistische Prosa,* ed. Karl Otten, Darmstadt, 1957, p. 21.

the meaning has not quite the same implications as in Werfel's already quoted verse: "Oh leise! Kein Ausbruch jetzt! Bebt! Schweigt!" For Hoelderlin, steeped in the classical heritage and in the critical philosophy of his day, artistic expression was not at all periods possible, only in moments of proximity to the gods (Götternähe).[6] These moments are distinguished from those of estrangement from the gods (Götterferne) by the transition from the "determined infinity of individuality" to the "universal infinity of the spirit and of light." This, forsooth, is not the language that would strike a sympathetic chord in the hearts of the generation that bled so profusely on the battlefields of Europe in 1914. With Hoelderlin the approach is basically a metaphysical one, characteristic of an age still guarded by idealistic absolutes and ideological constructs. Along with his contemporaries, Werfel could fall back on no such consolatory sanctions, sanctions which make Hoelderlin's already tottering world seem fairly stable when compared with our own. "The poet and the reader of poetry," Hofmannsthal had written in 1906, "no longer resemble the same persons in any other epoch of the past. For that the century from which we are extricating ourselves has heaped up the phenomena too strongly, and too powerfully fanned the spectral dance of mute appearances . . . ."[7] For Werfel and his generation the conflict was here and now, unleashed between man and his society. Furthermore, it is well to remember that Hoelderlin was possessed of a carefully pondered, if sometimes obscure, Sprachtheorie in relation to art, while it now seems clear that the expressionists displayed a relative failure to formulate the aesthetic of their art, despite their well-intentioned but vague manifestoes.[8]

It is not my purpose to evaluate Werfel's poetry as a whole—it has been well-done elsewhere—except to mention in passing Rilke's subtly provocative essay "Über den jungen Dichter" (1913), admittedly inspired by Werfel's first two verse-volumes. In many respects a Lobgesang on the literary accomplishments of the new generation of writers, the essay nevertheless voices a cautious warning. "And yet," writes Rilke, "who has not, for a moment at least, looked on with mistrust and asked himself whether it is really a matter of fruitfulness or only a mechanically better, more exhaustive exploitation of spirit? It [this age] confuses us with ever new visibilities, and to how much it has

6 Böckmann, Paul, op. cit., p. 262

7 Hofmannsthal, Der Dichter und diese Zeit, Stockholm, 1906, p. 292.

8 Michael Hamburger, Reason and Energy: Studies in German Literature, New York, 1957, p. 215.

already exposed us, for which there is no corresponding advance within ourselves." The passage sets up in bold relief, I believe—though in typically Rilkean formulation and from a different vantage point—the very scruples which Werfel was more and more to entertain regarding the use and misuse of poetic language, scruples which ultimately led him to concentrate on prose rather than poetry. It speaks highly for Werfel's integrity *precisely* as a poet that he subsequently turned to the cultivation of a genre which removed the obstacle of the poetic "Wortschuld."

It is therefore refreshing, in summary, to point to three Werfel poems, written at different intervals of time, since they not only reveal his still unflagging concern with the purity of the poetic word but also betray a trend toward greater structural simplicity and deeper spiritual maturation as time went on. The first poem is the allegorical "Das Licht und das Schweigen" ("Light and Silence") from *Der Gerichtstag* (1916-17). Here the primordial "unified light and silence" of creation is conceived as having been necessarily broken up and scattered in order to become incorporated in human love, as God became man in the Incarnation. It is the poet's task, in turn, to reconstruct out of the manifold sound and color elements the original pattern in the form of new silence and new song. From here to the next poem "Allelujah" *(Beschwörungen,* 1918-21 is only a step, since it supplies a variation on the light-theme of the preceding "Light and Silence," though it is less rhetorical and extravagant in expression, more simple and compact in form, and more lyrical with its effective Brentano-like refrain at the stanza-end:

> Ist das Licht nicht immer Eines,
> Wenn es auch durch Schwall und Schicht
> Bunt sich bricht,
> Kranker Abschein seines Scheines,
> Uns zur dumpfen Farbenwelt
> Sich zerschellt?
> Licht ist Licht!
>   Oh schweigendes Jauchzen!
> (Is the light not always One,
> Though but motley fracture
> Through the floods and layers of words,
> Sick reflection of its shining,
> Wrecks itself
> Into the dim color-world?
> Light is light!
>   O silent rejoicing!)

If the preceding poem had already explained how the original purity
of light came to be fractured and stained, "Allelujah" merely insists
that light is always one and unified, no matter what maculate trans-
formations it may be forced to undergo. The second stanza then proceeds to draw an analogy between this light and the human soul:

> Ist die Seele denn nicht Eines,
> Die sich dumpf in Körpern bricht,
> Und aus Auge und Gesicht
> Zuckt als Abschein ihres Scheines?
> Nur die Leiber
> Sind wie Scheiben
> Mehr und minder dicht.
>   Oh schweigendes Jauchzen!

> (Is the soul not always One,
> Though dimly fracturing in bodies,
> Mere reflection of its shining,
> Quivering from eye and face?
> But the bodies
> Are like glass-panes,
> Transparent more or less
>   O silent rejoicing!)

Here once again Werfel has picked up the "glass-pane" metaphor of
the early poem "The Poet" with which our discussion began. And,
finally, in "Legende von der Sprache" ("The Legend of Language")
from the collection *Hymnarium* written later than the others, Werfel
evolves his vision of language with even greater clarity in the direction
in which he had long been spiritually heading: the birth of the word
from the original Logos:

> Sprache ist an uns ergangen
> Vor des Lebens Wann und Wo.
> Unser Geist bleibt eingefangen
> Ewiglich im A und O...

> (Language was assigned to us,
> Before life's When and Where.
> In Alpha and Omega is
> Forever the spirit bound.)

In simple rhymed quatrains the poem proceeds to unfold the legend
of how, in the early earth-ages, the elders of the peoples *mutely* assem-

bled before their highest Lord whom they were unable to see because of the wall of hymnic flame that enclosed him. Suddenly, at a command, the three archangels emerge from the girdling fire and, each lifting his sword, hew from "the lava of song, from the Sanctus," piece by piece, original word and language in its integral purity, the kind of word and language—it would not be too much to say—that Franz Werfel envisioned as the goal of his ideal throughout his poetic practice.

ADOLF D. KLARMANN

Franz Werfel and the Stage

"The classical form of the mystery play is the struggle between God and the devil, which is decided in the human Ego." These words appear in an essay of which only a small part has been published, *Dramaturgie und Deutung des Zauberspiels "Spiegelmensch,"*[1] which Werfel's publisher Kurt Wolff printed in 1921 in a special limited edition of thirty copies and destroyed immediately afterward at the author's request.

The thirty-year-old author, whom the experiences of war had jolted from his ego-impregnated confidence in a world that redeemed itself into a deeper and more profound view, settles accounts with his vanities of madness and those of the world in his great mystery play *Spiegelmensch,* which unfortunately has been almost completely forgotten today. It is in this mystery play, which criticism at all levels has erroneously compared with Goethe's *Faust,* that he especially comes to terms with the vanities of reflected world boredom and self-satisfied salvationism, behind which the deceit of God attempts to hide itself. God and devil fight for the soul of man. Significantly Werfel calls his work "magic trilogy," and in his own commentary on it he labels it a "magic play." One notices a conscious avoiding of the terms drama, tragedy, play, or whatever the fitting traditional or customary title might be. The author seldom uses these terms without adding at least one qualifying word, e.g. "tragedy of a leader" for *Das Reich Gottes in Böhmen* or "romantic drama" for *Der Besuch aus dem Elysium.*[2]

A suggestion of the familiar aversion of expressionism toward outworn and threadbare forms is obvious, but does not give the completely adequate explanation of Werfel's definition. From the very beginning of his dramatic activity the author is very much concerned in needling the audience even more than the reading public out of their emotional sluggishness and complacency and making them aware of the differ-

[1] Dramaturgy and Interpretation of the Magic Play "Mirror Man."
[2] The Visit from Elysium.

ence in nature of his work which distinguishes it from that of a Schiller, Hebbel, Ibsen, and the naturalists, and also from his contemporaries of expressionism like Sorge or Hasenclever or Kornfeld, in whose works the hero, who is himself redeemer and world-judge, never feels a doubt of his own powers and authority.

With Werfel it is not a matter of pathetic conflicts of personality and world—rather his drama is carried out in the protagonist. It is plainly theological drama, as in the case of the Spaniards of the Golden Century whom he loved so much, and also in the case of Grillparzer and Hofmannsthal. The searching man is placed in the world in order to pass a probationary test before the omnipresent divine eye. As the master of his will, it is up to him to make the choice between good and evil. Whatever his choice may turn out to be, he stands under the shelter of the divine grace which can pardon the penitent and perform miracles of redemption on the lost. Imbued early with the Messianic mission of a literary work of art, he ascribes to it metaphysical interests which, to be sure, have to be clothed in a form which the public cannot easily understand, or maybe never understand at all. In his unpublished observations of 1928, *Ueber das Geheimnis der Kunst,*[3] there is the statement: "The value of a work of art—its weight in symbolism; its metaphysical ambiguity—its solid rooting in mystery. Greatest enemy—the knowing hint about it. (Classic example: my first dramas.)"

The substance of the drama is limited; on the other hand the ways to treat and develop it are of the greatest variety. Werfel knows, as did the Spaniards and also Shakespeare and on the other side Grillparzer and Raimund, that the lifeblood of the theater is entertainment and that the theatrical effect is not based on Lessing's or the French versions of Aristotelian concepts, but on the inner laws of the stage, which is neither a moral institution nor any other kind of institution, but again and again above all *Schau-Spiel,* show-play, spectacle. The twenty-two-year-old author had already written in his essay *Die Bühne von Hellerau:*[4] "The theater is the place where all serve one another in turn —actors and audience, light and author, music and chance—in order to form fanatically the whole which we call influence and effect. (Only quite shallow moralists do not know that the effect is one of the highest earthly things and is the oldest son of intensity.)" In the above quoted *Spiegelmensch* dramaturgy, the author laid down the three basic laws of the stage, namely:

[3] About the Secret of Art.   [4] The Stage of Hellerau.

    I. The law of the varied and richly significant situation.

   II. The law of the exciting and challenging possibilities for acting.

 III. The law of the sparkling and effervescing theatrical gesture and language.

And later: "The dramatist must mysteriously flatter the house. He must make the consciousness of the people on the other side of the prompter's box more godlike than that of the puppets on this side. He should mold not only the scene, but also the audience, for Schiller and the teachers of the theater are wrong—the stage has nothing to do with ethics—it is subtle incitement and temptation—at best toward that which is good."

From this metaphysically rooted autochthony of the stage, Werfel drew conclusions which have given his dramatic creations their own distinctive touch and they have not been without influence on his time and ours. As already in the expressionistic drama, the dramatic structure of the acts breaks down generally, even where it is still retained as in *Bocksgesang*. There is instead of this rather an "absence of form" as seen from the architectonic standpoint which grows from its own musical tectonics. In spite of the devotion to realism which Werfel emphasized again and again, the reader cannot be content with any kind of traditional definition of the term—certainly not at all with that familiar to the Naturalists from Zola and Ibsen on—much less with that of the "Neue Sachlichkeit." Perhaps the realism of an epic Brecht theater is closest anticipated here—in spite of its contrary position in all other respects—but, to be sure, entirely without his paralyzing didacticism.

In the observations on the drama *Juarez und Maximilian* there is this in addition: "To be sure the epic nature of the story—if it is not to be violated—prescribes a certain sequence of events, which often enough runs counter to the inexorable law of tragedy. However, from days of yore the dramatic story has always been a conscious form which tries to reconcile the conflict between drama and epic." For example, consider the drama *Das Reich Gottes in Böhmen* with its alternating main stage and proscenium, the latter almost always representing a road (in the early version of the drama stagehands appear with roadsigns!), or again the deeply moving pantomime before the fifth scene. In the same work Werfel uses the triptych form of the simultaneous stage, not only to represent the same historical room—in this case the Council of

Basle—but also toward the end to permit the widely separated figures of the Cardinal and Prokop to appear at the same time and in this way represent vividly and graphically the struggle for the brother's soul: "Two spotlight beams. On the right: high, open window. In front, Julian. On the left: a bed. On it the sick Prokop. Slow heavy ticking of an invisible pendulum." With these very characteristic stage directions we have already reached his suprarealism, i.e. a realism in which reality is crystalline so that the initiated not only can see through it, but understand it and also perceive its prismatic refraction. The foreground part of the stage action (and also that of the prose) is there to fascinate, to divert, to lead astray, to confuse and bewilder—or in a word—to become ironic; for that secret that is divulged is no longer a secret and becomes common knowledge. But neither God nor the poet make life that easy for man.

The frequent scenic exaggerations of his dramas are explained from this serious play instinct to give free rein to the theater magic of his baroque Austrian nature and feelings. This occurs in the early dramas such as *Spiegelmensch* or *Schweiger* and also in his last work for the stage, *Jacobowsky und der Oberst*. The Prague citizens Ach and Ichgereut or the incessantly chattering Drahomira call to mind a Shakespearean comedy, and Rosenberg is not merely by chance the namesake of Zawisch in Grillparzer's Ottokar-drama (all in *Das Reich Gottes in Böhmen*).

Actions concentrate at a strategic place as in the Spanish drama or again in Grillparzer—as in the scene at the execution place in the Paulus drama where at the critical moment in fateful presence almost every figure makes an appearance as if he were taking part in a divine revue. It is similar to the harbor tavern scene in the Jacobowsky play, this "comedy of a tragedy," where in the midst of the awful reality of the flight from the advancing Germans a holy Franciscan and the eternal Jew come riding up on a tandem bicycle.

It is just this last dramatic work of the author, completed under mental and emotional torments, that is an outstanding example of Werfel's suprarealistic art, the most obscure allegory, the most successful mystery play of the present in which, as in the Paulus drama, but with quite different previous suggestions and more conscious deception of the audience, the cosmic tragedy of the mission of the Christian and of the Jew is unrolled. The gentle symbolic hinting of the author extends to the naming of the characters. The stage directions—which in

this very case have developed to a highly cunning artistic device—
mysteriously hint at a great mystic event and transport the spectators
in the fate-filled last minute before the Last Judgment. Magic theater!

This has always been the case with Werfel!

Even the very first works—the fragments and the completed ones—
bubble over and sparkle with the magic of the theater: the fragment
Der Berg des Beginns,[5] festival cantata with scene and dance; the
"romantic drama" *Der Besuch aus dem Elysium;* the magic play *Die
Mittagsgöttin.* This theater magic reaches new heights in the "magic
trilogy" *Spiegelmensch* or in the depressing and yet hopeful, splendid
Bocksgesang. The musical basic experience, which gives the primary
form and which is familiar to those who know E. T. A. Hoffman, Kleist,
Grillparzer, and others, is amazing also in the case of Werfel. The first
idea for *Spiegelmensch* appears in the form of a ballet; at a Swiss per-
formance of *Die Troerinnen* he felt the operatic qualities in the piece,
and in *Der Weg der Verheißung*[6] text, pantomime, scenery, dance
(and Max Reinhardt) are combined with the music of Kurt Weill into a
veritable pageant. Magic, enchantment, theater, tricks and illusions,
overpowering thrills and excitement. Opera. Music! The drama of
Werfel arises from these various worlds and reaches the stage—that
which is opposed to reason and common sense and just because of that,
the real trueness of opera! The dramatist as librettist of the stage! (That
is what he once called Schiller.) For the boy in Prague the Italian
stagioni are the most exciting experience; until the end of his life Verdi
remained for him the divine singer, the man who set the human voice
free. He translated and prepared anew the libretto for three of his
operas and with that he ushered in Verdi's triumphant renaissance.

The fanatical interest in music in the works of Werfel is rooted deeply
in his mission of the eternal warning that *God is.* Out of this and
around this flows the music. It penetrates even into the innermost
structure of his work, in the duets of the contrasting couples which
complement each other to form a new unity, which, however, has always been theirs and was only temporarily separated, like two voices,
that going their way mingle with each other in a higher harmony. So it
is in the Paulus drama—the innermost, painfully blissful, intimate relationship of Gamaliel and Paulus, and Paulus and Chanan; or also Juarez
and Maximilian, Jacobowsky and Stjerbinsky, Julian and Prokop. Again

[5] The Mountain of Beginning.
[6] The Eternal Road.

and again there is also the polyphonic blending of sounds in the ensemble—as, for example, at the hanging place in *Das Reich Gottes in Böhmen,* or in the uniquely musically-conceived scene of the investing of the high priest in the temple on the eve of the Day of Repentance. In this scene Werfel even makes use of musical signs in the text. We can only point out, in passing, the countless examples of musical accompaniment for dramatic incidents. However, it is again and again the baroque Austrian joy in the theater, the ecstasy of the great situation, the overpowering scene, the confusing of sense and perspective in the complete adventure of the stage experience. It is to all of these that Werfel the dramatist succumbs, enjoying them as he contributes enjoyment.

It has already been indicated that the material is limited for an author who is engaged in metaphysical pursuits. Once Werfel even listed the areas of concern: "The mystic basic facts of the realm of spirits: creation of the world, the fall of man, incarnation, resurrection, etc." In the quite difficult cosmogony and eschatology of Werfel—the details of which we cannot discuss here—*revolt* stands out as perhaps the all-pervading characteristic feature. Even in the early lyrics of the searching youth, Lucifer plays a very important role, yet he is not conceived as the devil but as the Promethean fallen angel, the impatient fellow-sufferer for whom God's permanence is incomprehensibly long and far-removed. The Luciferian protest against the world of God-father, against the world of ancestors, is the breath of life of the early prose—*Nicht der Mörder, der Ermordete ist schuldig.* It becomes the symbol of ineradicable evil since the fall of man in the *tragodia, Bocksgesang* and in the prescient *Schweiger;* it leads to patricide and the most unpardonable of all sins, that against one's own seed, against the future, against the Messianic promise in *Spiegelmensch.* Rebellious accusation against the senseless order of the men's world is the martyrdom of *Die Troerinnen.*

Senseless order, the order also which contradicts common sense, can in man's limited view be chaos in which he, flattering himself with the conceit of a redeemer's mission, imagines himself called upon to bring about his own order, only to be dashed to pieces again and again on the order which is eternally incomprehensible to him and which hardly notices his efforts to shake it. That is the tragic fate of the well-meaning Hapsburger, Maximilian of Mexico, this touching figure of the self-appointed redeemer; that is also the end of the defiant leader of the Bohemians, Prokop, the Lord's fighter. Only in a fairy tale piece of fiction like *Jacobowsky und der Oberst* can the heathen proselyte Stjerbinsky in spite of his purely formal faith have a presentiment of the path of the genuine faith which he will enter upon with Jacobowsky, that is, the son of Jacob. The cardinal's prayer at the end of the drama *Das Reich Gottes in Böhmen* is true for all of them: "I love this dour and unyielding people ... Because of its rebellion ... For this rebellion, it too is a longing for You ...."

Not only rebellion against mighty Rome, not only against the god-given law—revolt against the Messianic mystery is the heart of the drama *Paulus unter den Juden,* which was to have been followed by two more parts, *Paulus unter den Heiden*[7] and *Paulus und Caesar,* as a trilogy of the Jewish-Christian mystery. It is incomprehensible to the Jew who believes strictly in the letter of the law that God would abandon his own work, his own house, that he would annul his word, that which is most holy of all. Inconceivable is the betrayal of Saul in the religious cause and the national awakening. The fanatical chauvinist Chanin, who loves Saul, plunges the land and people into Roman misery and hangs himself because in his own revolt against order he can no longer understand Saul's final humble and steadfastly confident revolt. Saul's conversion to Paul was the most damnable heresy to the rabbis. Even the loyal followers of Jesus, James and Peter, reject Paul's revolt against the exclusiveness of the Judeo-Christianity. Gamaliel is the only one to whom the significance of the Pauline enlightenment appears. He blesses the favorite pupil who has to abandon him, and then dies. The scapegoat has returned to the temple, the Anti-Messiah has appeared. The law is annuled. A new age of the fulfillment of the divine love has begun. The divine offer of the Messiah to the Jews has been rejected. With that they enter into a new order, a new mission. The word of God goes out among the heathen through Paul's mouth.

Mystery, probationary test, decline, the light of Parousia—these are the important elements in the drama *Paulus unter den Juden*—the show-play-spectacle.

[7] Paul Among the Heathen.

IAN C. LORAM

Franz Werfel's *Die Mittagsgöttin*

The expressionist revolt was born of an idealistic longing to sweep a dirty world clean with a new broom. Several elements which are now referred to as typically expressionist are common to other periods in German literary history when traditional, accepted values and norms came to be regarded as highly questionable. This in turn raised problems which were at once elementary and complex: good and evil, God and Man, to act or accept passively, and according to the bent or the natural talent of the individual these problems were treated simply or elaborately. This is evident in baroque literature and again in the literature of romanticism.

The expressionist's efforts to solve these problems, as far as the literary manifestations are concerned, are revealed in the ecstatic, often exaggerated, highly symbolic, ambiguous and frequently mystical manner of presentation. All of this is obviously apparent in the drama, and Franz Werfel, one of the most articulate and artistic representatives of the movement, is an example of the best and worst in this genre. The style and form of expressionism make it easy to carry it to extremes, leading often to a sterile futility, ridiculous in form and content; and Werfel occasionally is a victim of his own passionate enthusiasm. Many of the typical expressionist characteristics and doctrines are contained in one of his earliest plays *Die Mittagsgöttin (The Goddess of Midday)*. On the other hand, there are aspects of the play which one associates more particularly with Werfel than with other dramatists of the time, as the following analysis will attempt to illustrate.

Werfel's play first appeared in 1919 as the second part of the fourth book of *Der Gerichtstag (Judgment Day)*. It can, however, stand independently, and was in fact reprinted separately in 1923.[1] There are three major points, all of them typical of the young Werfel, which

[1] Franz Werfel, *Die Mittagsgöttin* (The Goddess of Midday): *Ein Zauberspiel* (Leipzig, 1923).

differentiate it from the Kaiser-Toller-Hasenclever type of drama. In
the first place, it is more obviously religious; second, it is considerably
more lyric in mood and technique; and third, it resorts occasionally to
a rather unpleasant brutality for shock effect. In addition, it is more
symbolically obscure.

The religious aspect of *Die Mittagsgöttin* is closely related to the
"new man" theme of expressionism, but Werfel uses a curious mixture
of pagan and Christian elements to make his point. The emphasis on
religion is not surprising when one considers Werfel's lifelong adher-
ence, however vague and uncertain it may have been, to the Judaeo-
Christian tradition. Since he was the most lyrical of the expressionist
writers who tried their hand at more than one genre, it is logical that
this too is reflected in the play. The shock technique can be attributed
to a youthful urge to express himself as vividly as possible, as well as
inexperience and lack of tact.

As we shall see, the play is a complex expression of man's longing—
indeed, his need—to find his way back to the origins of life.[2] This
journey is absolutely necessary in order that he may begin to shape
himself anew by casting off the shackles and false trappings of his
present existence. He must be reborn in his pristine, i.e. pure and absolute or essential form. The recovery of this purity, referred to again and
again as "white light" means for Werfel that the divine has manifested
itself and that all things are one in the divine. In a poem entitled "Der
gute Mensch" ("The Good Man," 1915) he wrote:

> Und wo er steht und seine Hände breitet,
> Und wo sein Ruf tyrannisch niederdonnert,
> Zerbricht das Ungerechte aller Schöpfung,
> Und alle Dinge werden Gott und eins.
>
> (And where he stands, extending wide his hands,
> Where his tyrannic call goes thundering down,
> There crash creation's gross injustices,
> And all becomes as God, and one.)[3]

The baroque mysticism and ecstatic longing reveal themselves in the
symbolic synthesis of erotic and religious yearning and experience, as
well as in the Christian desire for martyrdom and suffering. In another

[2] In a later play, *Bocksgesang* (Goat Song), one of the characters longs to return
to a state of "original chaos."
[3] Franz Werfel, *Poems,* trans. Edith Abercrombie Snow (Princeton, 1945),
p. 33.

early poem Werfel begged: "Begnade mich mit Martern, Stich um Stich!" ("Redeem me with torture, thrust by thrust!"), and although this theme is more restrained in *Die Mittagsgöttin,* we shall see that the need for suffering is still in evidence.

The protagonist of Werfel's theme is Laurentin, a tramp, who is Man, none too subtly disguised in his dusty clothes and shoes, with a bundle on his back. In a Faustian monologue he deplores his inadequacy and his inability to find "peace and rest." He recognizes, or thinks that he recognizes, the source of his trouble: "Weil in mir eine Heimat lebt, Die ewig außer mir mein Fuß anstrebt." ("Because *within* me there exists a haven, toward which I am forever striving *externally.*") He is endeavoring to realize his inner self, but despite all efforts, remains externally oriented. This discovery of the inner self is a step on the way back to the absolute, but cannot be achieved by desire alone. "Der Autor . . . zeigt jetzt den expressionistischen Menchen in seinem Verhältnis zu einer gotthaltigen Wirklichkeit, in seiner Läuterung auf das Göttliche hin, in seiner Erlösung in das Göttliche hinein . . . . Die Faustnaturen treten wieder auf, die Sucher nach dem Absoluten." ("The author shows the expressionistic man in his relationship to a divine reality, in his purification through striving for the divine, in his redemption within the divine . . . . The Faustian natures appear again, the seekers of the absolute.")[4] Laurentin indicates that love may be the solution to the problem, but his "uneinige Geister" (dissenting spirits) prevent him from finding it. Like Faust, it has occurred to him to try magic, but he has rejected it as a "desert." Each time that he has attempted to find himself through love, he has failed. "Die Liebe wird mager, bekommt das Mieseln." ("Love becomes thin and anaemic.") In this same monologue he touches upon a major symbol of the play: the contrast between colored light and white light. Colors represent the undesirable, perhaps because they are the result of the diffusion of an essential, basic element into a number of less clear, hence more distracting parts. Man is not yet capable of wholehearted dedication to one goal, but diffuses his energy in "Blendwerk—und Prismen-Spiel" ("a delusive and prismatic show"). "Und er [Expressionismus] verlangte... die Heimkehr aus dem Vielfältigen in das Einfache, Ursprüngliche, zu Kindheit, Urzustand und Paradies." ("It [Expressionism] demanded the return from multiplicity to simplicity, to the origin of things, to child-

---

[4] Otto Mann, in *Expressionismus,* hrsg. Hermann Friedmann und Otto Mann (Heidelberg, 1956), p. 226.

hood, the pristine state and Paradise.")[5] Laurentin longs to reunite
these spectrum colors into their original concentrated form, and in so
doing to discover his own essence.

As he lies sleeping at the side of the road, exhausted by his wander-
ing, Mara, the goddess, appears in the nearby field of ripe corn. We see
her through his eyes as he awakens and describes her. She is "golden,"
like the corn, and the sunflower which she carries is her sceptre and her
symbol. She has felt Laurentin's need and appears to aid him, half
solicitous, half reproachful:

> Am Ort der Reife ist durch dich gestört
> Das Wandelnde, das ineinander paßt . . .
> So ist der Ort des Werdens irritiert,
> Weil du in einem bösen Pendel schwingst.
>
> (In the place of ripeness you have disturbed
> The transforming power which welds together . . .
> The place of becoming is upset,
> Because you whirl in an evil oscillation.)

Mara looks in vain for a sign of suffering in his face. She finds it pure,
but this purity is sinful:

> Denn ein Mal
> Dein Antlitz trägt: Der hier verwarf die Qual.
> Es hat dies Haupt den Dornen nicht getraut,
> Sich nicht der Kraft ergeben, welche baut,
> Und nie geliebt!
> (For your face
> Bears a sign: this man spurned suffering.
> This head did not know the crown of thorns,
> Did not surrender to the power that builds,
> And has never loved!)

Laurentin resents the accusation and, in a complicated series of images
and word-plays, compares himself to the beam of a lighthouse which
picks up a sail at sea. The sail is essential reality and he projects himself into it, hoping thereby to create—or recreate—himself:

> Sein Schaffen liebend, liebt er, was er schuf.
> Liebt im Geschaffenen sein Schaffen nur,
> Im Ding das Ding, aus dem er sich erfuhr . . .

[5] Fritz Martini, *Was war Expressionismus?* (What was Expressionism?)
(Urach, 1948), p. 24.

(Loving his creative power, he loves what he created.
In that which has been created he loves only his creative power,
In the thing only that thing by which he experienced himself.)

But the sail inevitably moves beyond the radius of the light, and he remains frustrated. Mara explains that there exists a "boy-god," whom we may interpret as Eros, who can be freed from his prison by one who loves, but Laurentin declares that he is searching only for the god who held himself aloof from his world. In other words, he is seeking the god of the orthodox, who created the world and then withdrew from it. Mara tells him that she comes from "Arabia, the land of the dawn" to help one who does not really exist. She is "midday" and "fountain of creation," searching for someone who has never belonged to her. Once Laurentin admits that he is not yet "a human being," Mara kisses him, and this arouses a peculiar longing to return to his point of origin, away from "false colors." After a third kiss she bids him "come home" and envelops him in her cloak so that he is invisible. This is so obviously the symbolic return to the womb before the rebirth that Laurentin's description of himself now as "zierlich und klein" ("delicate and small") and his plea "O knüpfe nur/Die Schnur um meinen kleinen Leib" ("O, bind the cord about my tiny body") are not only quite unnecessary, but almost ludicrous.

Night falls, and Mara awaits the birth of her child. This is "the hour of my weakness," when the magical strength of noon is almost exhausted; it is a time of darkness, evil, fear, and danger. Midday, with the sun at its zenith, is the source of her power: the warmth, the brilliance and all the properties which make for growth, fruition, and maturity. Werfel carries on the symbolic pattern as a gendarme appears with a warrant for Laurentin's arrest, charging him with espionage and claiming that he is "insgeheim mit der Entente im Bund" ("secretly in league with the Entente"). This figure represents those forces which are dangerous because they are prosaic, philistine, and reactionary—hostile to change because they cannot understand it. Since Laurentin is symbolically in Mara's womb, and literally hidden beneath her cloak, the gendarme must admit failure.

A funeral passes by, and Mara learns that a young mother who died in childbirth is to be buried. She died because "she did not know how to wait, spent her time in drudgery and did not rest." Mara then resolves to wait properly, feeling all about her the power of evil, which is determined to destroy her and the unborn child. This evil force, which is dependent upon estrangement from God, recognizes in every seed the attempt of the divine to manifest itself and seeks to annihilate it.

The ultimate evil then makes its appearance in the form of the *Abdecker* (flayer of horses). He is Werfel's conception of the final destructive force, a kind of death, swinging a whip instead of a scythe, with a bony nag pulling his wagon:

> Ich aber bin die Feindschaft alles Trächtigen,
> Der wache Fuhrmann,
> Der gut auslugt und paßt,
> Daß nicht ins Einige entwische,
> Was hier zerfallen sein muß!
> Drum weh dem Vollendenden,
> Wehe dem hoffend Wachen,
> Das mir begegnet
> Zu meiner Stunde.
> Es muß mir unter die Plache.

> (I am that which is hostile to everything pregnant,
> The vigilant driver
> Who keeps a sharp lookout,
> And takes care
> That nothing which must disintegrate here
> Escapes into unity!
> Therefore woe to that
> Which is in the process of consummation,
> Woe to the hopeful waking which encounters me
> When my time is ripe.
> It must fall under my wagon traces.)

It would seem, however, that this destructive force is not something of external origin, but is within man, symbolic of the petty and often fatal weaknesses which prevent him from fulfilling himself:

> Ich bin der Herr
> Des kleinen Fehlers,
> Der Fürst des unendlichen
> Dezimalbruchs,
> Feind aller Lösung.

> (I am the master
> Of the little fault,
> The lord of the infinite
> Decimal fraction,
> Enemy of all solution).

He will wait with Mara, pitting his strength against hers. As he begins his destructive work, Laurentin, in his dark refuge, is at once afraid. Mara has no defense except to sit quietly, hoping that her contemplation of what she knows is beautiful will give her the power to resist. The object of this contemplation is the burgeoning life within her, and it gradually restores her strength to the point where she is able to combat, with her own swarms of bees and butterflies, the symbolic owls and bats which accompany the flayer. She is only temporarily successful, since her adversary has not yet exhausted his resources and (here Werfel's shock technique comes into play) reveals to her what is on his wagon. "Auf einer Schicht von Tierkadavern liegen Menschenleichen. Starre Glieder hängen über den Rand; dazwischen regen sich Betrunkene. Kranke heulen leise und zeigen auf ihre Beulen, ein Aussätziger klappert, ein Wahnsinniger plappert, an allem auf und nieder huschen rasche Ratten." ("Corpses lie on a layer of dead animals. Rigid limbs project over the edge; between them drunken figures move. Diseased people moan softly and display their sores, a leper swings his clapper, a madman babbles, and rats slip swiftly all about.") This, he tells Mara, is the true picture, this the real dream of hope, and he bids her give up and follow him. But she still resists and refuses to be afraid, because she knows that even should she be defeated "Doch immer lebt ein Weib nach mir/Das es vollbringen wird" ("inevitably some woman will come after me who will fulfill this destiny").

The enemy makes his supreme effort. He drags a bloody misshapen foetus from his wagon and holds it up to Mara. Here, he shouts, is "die große Zukunft" ("the great future"), this is the true Christ. But day is approaching and with it Mara's sphere of influence. She now begins to feel the first birth pangs, and as Laurentin calls her loudly by name from within his refuge her labor begins. The flayer and his ghastly retinue disappear—defeated. Laurentin, bloody, scratched, breathless, appears suddenly from the thickets. He has come "durch endlose Urwaldnacht" ("through endless night in the primeval forest") seeking Mara. She sends him for help in her hour of need. Both the physical appearance of Laurentin and the logical symbolic sequence imply that he has now been born again.

This is not enough, however. Laurentin is suffering, which is one condition of rebirth, but he has not loved, so that he is still confused, runs in circles, and only when he falls on his knees and prays, confessing that "Ich habe keine selbstgefälligen Tränen mehr" ("I can no

longer weep self-complacent tears") and that he knows now what love
is, does he find help in the form of peasants who have come to work the
fields. (Worth noting here is that it is the simple, rural type which
offers assistance, part of the romantic tradition in Expressionism.) As
they are about to set out to find Mara, she appears, carrying a male
child in her arms. It is not a newborn babe. She tells Laurentin that he
is beginning all over again, and announces that the child is his son.
However, it and not he is pure. "Rein ist nur das Begonnene!" ("Only
the inchoate is pure!") Laurentin kneels before the child, in reality
kneeling before his new self and the divine in himself. The result of the
entire process has been:

> Aus Farben zu erwachen!
> In Weißheit einzugehen!
> (To emerge from the world of color!
> To enter the realm of pure white light!)

Laurentin asks whether that which is eternally yet to be, the essence
of hope is the forgiving God. Mara avoids an immediate answer and
warns him again that they must part, when the gendarme appears and
tries to arrest Laurentin. However, with a touch of her sunflower Mara
transforms him into a hermit in a monk's habit, giving him the flower,
now turned into a tiny lantern, to guide him. The gendarme has to retire
in the face of this miracle, and, with a wry sense of humor, asks:

> Denn eine Kutte arretieren,
> Wer wagte so etwas in Österreich?
> (Who would dare be so rash
> As to arrest a monk in Austria?)

Laurentin must pass the rest of his days in solitude, but Mara con-
soles him by saying that hope is the essence of the ultimate power. It is
perhaps not carrying things too far to say that the child represents
"hope"—the hope of the world. Mara then disappears, and Laurentin
turns into the woods to live out his life in a hut provided for him by the
old peasant. "Die Welt," says Laurentin, "ist ein abgestammeltes
Gerücht, das dem Schöpfer aus dem Sinn gekommen ist. Ich will
denken, ich will denken, bis der schwere Stein meines Ichs zur stetig
weißen Flamme wird, bis meine Farben wieder vereint sind ins heilig-
einfach Weiße, meine Worte gesammelt ins Schweigen, dann will ich
Gott erinnern und ihm sein Rätsel zuschweigen." ("The world is a fal-
tering rumor which the creator has forgotten. I shall contemplate, I shall

ponder, until the heavy stone of my ego becomes a flame which shall always burn white, until my colors are again fused into a simple, sacred whiteness, until my words are gathered into silence. Then I shall take God into myself and cover his mystery with my silence.")

Like many expressionist plays which concern themselves primarily with the "new man," we see that the end does not bring a solution. Rather, it presents only the hope of solution: the protagonist sees the way, but time is still needed before he can fulfill his task, before the world is ready to accept what he has to offer. Laurentin is no exception. The process by which he arrives at his rebirth is a complicated one, and the way which lies before him will not be easy. Werfel adds a new note to what we have come to regard as conventional Expressionism by the introduction of the supernatural. While some expressionist plays still contain elements of naturalism, Werfel departs radically from it by presenting the magical as visible. For a time the real, in the form of Laurentin, is literally hidden within the unreal, but this is no more paradoxical for Werfel than the way in which he eliminates time barriers. Mara is pagan because she is a magical phenomenon. But more than this, she represents the origin of things, both the "natural" source of everything which is created and which matures, and the abstract religious concept of rebirth through love, hope, and faith. She comes, significantly enough, from that part of the earth where civilization may very well have originated, long before Christianity was known. When the flayer taunts her with the bloody foetus as "the true Christ" he is anticipating the future, but since the play takes place in the present, time means nothing to Werfel here. Similarly, when Mara bears the child, time boundaries are again eliminated, since the child represents the divine in man, that which is yet to be realized. The resemblance between Mara and the Madonna, not to mention the similarity in the names Mara and Maria, is unmistakably intentional. Werfel attempts to remove the apparent paradox that Laurentin is both creator and created by the elimination of temporal restrictions. "Werfel haßt und verwirft das Tote und Starre der Zeit" ("Werfel detests and rejects the deadness and rigidity of time"), says Martini,[6] and in Laurentin's opening monologue he admits that one of the reasons he has not been able to find peace is because he is filled with a sense of time.

The theme of suffering and torture as a means of finding the ultimate solution is a favorite of Werfel's. It is, in *Die Mittagsgöttin,* not only

[6] Martini, p. 147.

something which Laurentin must discover (because that which he has
assumed to have been suffering is not), but he must welcome it and
attempt to lose himself in it—it should become almost a pathological
necessity. This is carried through the play; at the end, as we have seen,
he is denied his plea to have Mara and the child remain with him. More
than that, he is destined to spend his life alone, until such time as mankind is ready to receive him. "Ich muß den toten Stein in meiner Seele
zum Schmelzen bringen. Ich muß das Schwere vollbringen, mich selbst
nicht mehr zu fliehen . . . . Wenn Gott mir hilft, werde ich euch einmal
willkommen sein dürfen." ("I must melt the dead stone in my soul. I
must fulfill the difficult task of no longer fleeing from myself . . . . If God
helps me, I will one day be allowed to receive your welcome.")

The religious element is unmistakable throughout—the search for the
divine and the absolute, the symbolism of Mara and the child, rebirth
as a step toward freeing the world, Laurentin as hermit and penitent,
the emphasis on the pure white flame. Even the flayer, as the protagonist of all that is at odds with itself, all that militates against the
achievement of a harmonious unity which is of divine origin, is part of
the religious tradition. This is further intensified by the strongly lyrical
mood. Here we find the same rhapsodic, hymnic element which is
characteristic of the young Werfel's poetry. Even at the end, where
prose replaces verse, it is of such a quality that we may call it hymnic.
It is true, however, that one is compelled to see this at times as ecstatic
enthusiasm, as part of the tradition that leads from the mystics of the
fourteenth century through Klopstock to Rilke. One cannot help but
feel that Werfel lets his fervor run away with him, giving in to the
temptation to express himself as absolutely as possible without much
regard for what he actually wishes to convey. "Für den expressionistischen Dramatiker wird entscheidend, daß er im Grunde beides verloren
hat, theologische und philosophische Bildung, und daß es seine Philo-
sophie ist, ein wohlgemeinter persönlicher Enthusiasmus könnte dieses
Verlorengegangene ersetzen." ("A decisive factor for the expressionist
playwright is the loss of both his theological and philosophical heritage.
His philosophy then consists of replacing both by a well-meant personal
enthusiasm.")[7]

The language of the play illustrates perhaps better than that of any
other expressionist the belief in the power of the word. Not the ecstatic
cry, not the animal-like ejaculation, not the silent pantomime, but the

[7] Mann, p. 234.

word is the expressive (sometimes over-expressive) element in *Die Mittagsgöttin*. Werfel is at times overcome by his ability to use and coin words, and he indulges in the kind of compound and invention which are part and parcel of the expressionist stock-in-trade. "Kreisel-Schein" (whirling illusion), "Strahlens-Wisser" (he who knows radiance), "Ur-Allein" (the original state of being alone), "unwiederbürtlich" (incapable of rebirth), "Leicht-Schwere Glorien-Schwebe" (light-heavy hovering glory) are typical. There are also several rather unfortunate figures of speech. For example: "Du wandelst auf meinem schiffbaren Blut." ("You are walking on my navigable blood.") Or, when Laurentin says: "Mara! In deinem Namen ist viel A" ("There is the sound of A in your name"), she replies: "So stimm dein Instrument an mir." ("Then tune your instrument with me.") One cannot, however, help admiring Werfel's ability and facility to move effortlessly from one rhythmic form to another. Whether he is using prose or verse there is a dynamic quality to his writing, and no one can doubt the sincerity of his style, however exaggerated and exhausting it may become. The errors of inexperience and the urge to say it all are, nevertheless, too evident to ignore. The funeral scene in the second act is forced and unnecessary and leads nowhere. The motif of the "boy-god" is dropped before it has time to develop. Most irritating of all is the laboriously complicated symbolic pattern which Werfel tries to weave. The attempt to portray Laurentin as both creator and created does not quite come off, due largely to Werfel's naive and awkward handling of the sexual implications.

The object of the search in *Die Mittagsgöttin* is a cosmic phenomenon, the divine or "humanity" (since for Werfel they are identical), contained both within man and outside of him. Until Laurentin becomes aware of this, he never knows whether it is reality or dream. His external world, which he may sometimes conceive of as real, is more frequently a dreamlike conception of his inner world. He does not know at first that the supernatural can be both pagan and Christian, and therefore calls Mara heathen. Nor does he realize that the religious and erotic experiences can be merged, so that when Mara speaks ecstatically of "Leib, Blut, Wein und Brot" ("body, blood, wine and bread") this is not incongruous by expressionist standards. His attitude toward reality is conditioned by his longing to find himself, and this, almost paradoxically, means finding the absolute in order to lose himself in it. He does this by returning literally and figuratively to man's point of origin. His son is a symbolic representation not only of his new self, but also the eternal faith, love, and hope which this new self has created. In this dream world of the absolute Werfel was seeking to work out the problems which haunted him and which he felt haunted the world, to realize that which in himself was not capable of realization. It is his expression of a desperately serious attempt to free himself and mankind, an attempt which was never to be successful, but which he was compelled to express in poetry, prose, and drama.

FRANK LAMBASA

Franz Werfel's *Goat Song*

In his remarkably sensitive portrayal of Franz Werfel and his work, Richard Specht named the play *Bocksgesang (Goat Song)* as one of the two works of Werfel that were generally considered as an outright artistic failure.[1] Written immediately after his metaphysically oriented verse trilogy, the *Spiegelmensch (Mirror Man)*, it experienced a slight theatrical debacle after it was given a double premiere in March 1922, in the theaters of Frankfurt and Vienna.[2] Most critics dismissed the play as a weird concoction of a revolutionary play and a social drama, of myth and folklore. But scholars, too, who delight in disentangling literary puzzles, and who had written extensively about other works of Werfel, seemed as if intentionally to avoid this particular play.[3] It may be finally added that the poet himself while preparing the first collected edition of his works deliberately excluded his *Goat Song* from the collection of his plays, thus passing, as it were, a judgment of unworthiness over it.[4] Was this attitude of critics as well as of the poet himself justified; is this consignment to oblivion of one of Werfel's major works warranted; does this play possess any merits, and does it have anything to say to us today: questions that still need to be answered.

[1] Richard Specht, *Franz Werfel: Versuch einer Zeitspiegelung*, P. Zsolnay Verlag, Berlin-Wien-Leipzig, 1926, p. 235: "Unter allen Werken Franz Werfels gibt es eigentlich nur zwei erfolglose: das Schauspiel "Bocksgesang" und den letzten der Gedichtsbände, die Beschwörungen."

[2] Uraufführung gleichzeitig am Wiener Raimundtheater und in Frankfurt a.M. In Wien ein Scheinerfolg (im Respekt des Nichtverstehens), in Frankfurt ein verhüllter Mißerfolg. Das Drama wartet bis heute seines szenischen Nachschöpfers." Specht, *op. cit.*, p. 323.

[3] While there are articles on practically anything that Werfel wrote, *Bocksgesang* (Goat Song) remains the stepchild of the critics. Even the admiringly complete work of Adolf D. Klarmann, *Franz Werfel: Gesammelte Werke, Die Dramen (Erster Band)*, S. Fischer Verlag, 1959, with its extensive annotations about other plays of Werfel, devotes only five and a half lines to the *Goat Song*. All German quotations from the play are from this edition.

[4] Franz Werfel, *Gesammelte Werke*, Paul Zsolnay Verlag, 1929.

The *Goat Song* was, after all, not only the first, full-length drama written in prose by Werfel, but it was also the one which made his name known in America. It had a distinction of being one of the first works which were to open a window across the Atlantic on the after-war mind of Germany's young and promising men of literature. Its fifty-eight performances on Broadway during the 1925-26 theater season, with Lynn Fontanne and Alfred Lunt in the leading roles and the brilliant settings by Lee Simonson, were considered only a mild success.[5] Though some critics went as far as to call it "the most important play of the season,"[6] the American theater audience and the critics in general were just as puzzled by its dramatic complexities, its cryptic obscurities, its symbolism and ambiguity, as were their German colleagues.

In attempting to cast a backward glance, however, couldn't we state that the time in which the *Goat Song* appeared was not yet ripe for it? Accustomed, after all, to plays that used to show clear-cut conflicts in character and event and idea, i.e. the issues which can quickly involve the sympathies and partisanship of the spectators, most people appeared to be baffled and irritated[7] by the play's complex and intricate pattern, by its perplexing contradictions which exist in this play far more than in any other work by Werfel. Today, on the other hand, after experiencing plays by such avant-garde playwrights as Adamov, Beckett, Ionesco, Dürrenmatt, etc., precisely these qualities of equivocation and a far-ranging ambiguity as far as its meaning is concerned seem to lend to this play a singularity which is emotionally as well as intellectually exciting. Seen in these terms, it could almost be asserted that one play by Werfel that would stand a chance of a revival and success would be his *Goat Song*.[8]

[5] It was produced by the Theatre Guild under the direction of Ben Ami with a cast of almost a hundred actors. The role of the Jew was played by the now famous movie actor Edward G. Robinson.

[6] Stark Young in *The New Republic* (Feb. 24, 1926).

[7] Brooks Atkinson, who was then the drama critic of *Vogue*, writes in a lengthy review: "That is the bare story as accurately as I could absorb it. It may mean many things. Milič says, 'Everything eternal fears fulfillment' [Atkinson is wrong here: Juvan, the student, says this!]—perhaps that's the idea. Or, maybe, merely, 'Life goes on.' Or—a thousand other things. I am conscious of a certain irritation that Herr Werfel does not tell us. There is no reason to obscure its meaning, yet he appears to have done just that, and deliberately. My irritation is so great that I am tempted to be facetious and dub 'Goat Song' 'The Scentaur,'" *Vogue* (March 1926).

[8] Heinz Beckmann wrote recently in *Rheinischer Merkur* (April 8, 1960), p. 21, in a review of Franz Werfel's early dramas: "Es ist recht merkürdig, daß man bei

The above statement does not arbitrarily set apart the play *Goat Song* from other works of Werfel, with an implication that it is not an integral part of his artistic tradition, or, that it does not fit within the frame of his so much discussed metaphysical outlook. It simply attempts to underline the fact that Werfel's philosophy—which is at the core of all of his works—is here much more broadly and ambiguously stated than in his other works, and this to its advantage rather than disadvantage. For the efficacy of the modern theater, at least, seems not to depend so much on the saturation of it with a certain *Weltanschauung* as much as on a certain ambiguity which permits individual interpretations no matter how contradictory they may sometimes appear to be. And it is true, that with no other work of Werfel there could be more contradictory interpretations as in the case of this play.[9]

Its title already alludes to a broad set of meanings: Its German name "Bocksgesang" is a direct translation from the Greek word "τραγῳδία" which literally means "goat song." This word, however, is also the Greek word for tragedy, deriving its name from the worship of Dionysius and his goatlike followers. This intentional play on words with its twofold reference to a ritualistic catharsis (rite becoming drama), on the one hand, and a literal story of the life, escape, and death of a monstrous goatlike freak on the other, suggests that the play itself can either be taken literally or understood as a huge dramatic symbol.

And the *Goat Song* dramatic plot is a fascinating one. Its scene is laid in "a Slav country beyond the Danube," at the end of the eighteenth and the beginning of the nineteenth century;[10] and it is built around a story allegedly reported in the press: "A monster was born to a rich peasant family—creature half beast, half man. The parents regarded it as a deep disgrace to the race of which they were proud and kept the

---

all dem Unfug, den man augenblicklich auf unseren Bühnen 'experimentiert,' noch nirgends auf den Einfall gekommen ist, es wieder einmal mit den früheren Dramen von Franz Werfel zu versuchen, mit dem 'Schweiger' vor allem, *auch mit dem 'Bocksgesang'* [my italics] oder gar mit dem 'Spiegelmensch' . . . ."

[9] Joseph Wood Krutch stated in *The Nation* (Feb. 17, 1926), while discussing Werfel's *Goat Song:* "His story is told in the most straightforward of manners, and it is vivid enough to constitute its own ambiguous air of relevance which clings about every thrilling legend and which gives the story of Hamlet or Don Juan as many meanings as there are imaginations to interpret it." (Theatre Section)

[10] It is interesting that Werfel, as in many other cases, had intuitively chosen the right period, historically speaking. There actually was a bloody rebellion in Serbia in the beginning of the nineteenth century which was also put down by the Janissaries just as in Werfel's play.

monster a secret, hiding it in a hovel on the estate, until it grew to maturity. Finally, it escaped, causing a social upheaval in the village."[11] With this as a central theme, Werfel has built up a drama in which traditional myths and folk tales, social and human passions, class war and rebellion are richly interwoven and interpenetrated with individual tragedies of love, hate, and anguish.

A rich landowner, Stevan Milič, according to the Werfel drama, is about to marry his son Mirko to the daughter of a neighbor, and the girl is to be left at her new home until the wedding. Stanja, the future bride, is troubled by the presence on the farm of a dog-kennel-like stable made of tile from which smoke ascends out of a chimney during the cold season. The groom, Mirko, tries to evade the girl's inquisitive probings. From childhood, he says, that has been the forbidden place of fear. Questioning father or mother was not permitted.

From the parents and the physician who visits them we learn that twenty-three years ago the wife gave birth to a monster, which neither she nor her husband has ever looked at, but which she has passionately loved, more, in fact, than her other normal son. On the day of Mirko's betrothal, Stevan, his father, decides to kill this monstrous creature and remove the blight from his son's future. The physician begs to be allowed to take away this beast, this "biological-anatomical-physiological miracle," as he calls it, to some institution suited to the purpose. The parents, however, fear the discovery of their shame; the mother also refuses to give up what she loves. The doctor, who assisted at its birth, goes now to inspect the monster. At the sight of it, however, he becomes completely disconcerted. "The ancients," he says, "believed that at high noon something could spring from quivering nature, formless but visible, horrible and full of majesty, blasting all that crossed it, like the vision of the Whole compressed into a second . . . ."[12] When the father

[11] *The Literary Digest* (Feb. 13, 1926), p. 25, quotes this passage indicating also that Werfel heard of the case in a Serbian village where he was stationed as a soldier during the First World War. It is interesting to note that a few other *American* critics quote the same source while *German* critics cite another one. Thus Annemarie von Puttkamer in her *Franz Werfel: Wort und Antwort*, p. 37, suggested that Werfel found inspiration "als er im Krüppelheim des Prager Vyschehrad eine bocksähnliche menschliche Mißgeburt mit hornartigen Auswüchsen über der Stirn und in schamloser Gebärde erblickte." Similarly Adolf Klarmann, *op. cit.*, p. 553, in his notes on *Bocksgesang:* "Den Prototyp des Bockes sah Werfel schon in früher Jugend bei einem Besuch des Pathologischen Instituts des Professor Jedlička auf dem Višehrad in Prag."

[12] The translation is by Ruth Langner (*Goat Song, The Theatre Guild An-*

goes to put it to death, he finds that the doctor, in his terror, has forgotten to lock the door and the monster has escaped.

Here the "fate and family drama," the private grief of the Milič household, swells into a torrent of a universal revolution. For in the second act we see a council of landowners before whom is brought the question of the landless, the outcasts, and the emigrants who are flooding the country and are demanding their share of it. Trouble threatens because the assembled elders reject the plea of these destitute paupers for food and land. Stevan Milič, the richest landowner, enters with his gun, completely frenzied over the disappearance of his monstrous child. He is deaf to everything but his own fear and shame. The old servant who has nursed the monster comes to say that there is still no trace of it. Stevan, half demented, chases out at gun point the representatives of the landless and rushes out to the hunt.

The third act shows the outcasts, their revolutionary dreams, their wild superstitions. Juvan, the solitary, misanthropic student-tramp, son of a village prostitute, who has returned to the scene of his childhood, becomes their leader. Stanja and her betrothed, Mirko, come to the place of the tramps' hideaway on the insistence of the girl, and it is seen that she and Juvan, in spite of their heated and scornful altercation, are in love with each other. Juvan leads the vagrants in a desperate insurrection when the escaped beast, whose great shadow suddenly hovers over them, is seized upon as an inspiration and a mystic symbol of a redeeming god. After they capture it, they leash it behind the Ikonostasis, the high altar of a Greek Orthodox village church. The deranged mob pillages the land and then comes to the church to worship "the sacred divinity" in a mixture of Greco-Latin and Church-Slavonic with all the frenzied madness of an ancient pagan ritual. Juvan is the self-acclaimed prophet of this "god," and a fantastic diakon by the name of Bogoboj is his priest. At the height of this grotesque mass, Juvan dares Stanja to go behind the altar and confront the monster. Her betrothed Mirko, in a frantic attempt to prevent this, is killed. But Stanja goes, and the passionate, rapturous cry of the unseen as she submits to its embrace sounds in triumph.

The play rushes now to its denouement: the countryside is laid waste before the Janissaries come to rout the rebels; the monster plunges into the burning forest and is consumed; Juvan, the leader, must pay with

thology, Random House, New York, 1936, pp. 394-438). Wherever the stage adaptation departs from the original, I substituted my own translation.

his life for conducting the uprising; the old order is restored, but Stevan Milič and his wife are reduced to solitude and poverty. Stanja, however, against the wishes of her parents, who would like to marry her off to another rich landowner, elects to remain with Stevan Milič and his wife. When Mirko's mother protests that the marriage was not consummated and that she is free to go home to her folks, Stanja refuses. She replies that her place is with them, because she belonged to their son. Life had entered her when she had gone into the Holy of Holies behind the altar, a voluntary immolation to the beast. She announces now that she is to bear the monster's child.

It is not surprising to hear after this necessary and rough outline of its dramatic content that most critics were mystified by this play. It was suspected, however, that behind the mere plot and all the theatrical devices of which Werfel was generally very fond, there were mystical undercurrents, hidden profundities, vague and devastating associations. The basic content, of course, is tragic action which Werfel directly presents. But this action is in its very essence ambiguous, so that each and every element of the play becomes readily transmutable into some sort of a symbol. In order that the symbolic level of the play be better understood, it is indispensable to know at least some of Werfel's metaphysical ideas.

The world into which man is born is essentially meaningless, asserts Werfel in one of his earliest pronouncements about the nature of tragedy.[13] Impulse and Accident rule all things, while Reason (or Intelligence), that fearful distinction of man alone, is asked to stand unshaken before the brutal drama of the elements. Yet from this disjunction between Man and Nature springs tragedy, a spark which leaps from the pole Reason or Sensibility to the pole called Life or Accident. The tragic sentiment exists because an original sin in which the entire nature shares must be atoned by man alone. And it is this accusation that the understanding, sensitive soul of humanity brings against fate that makes the core of tragedy, and yet this tragic sentiment alone is capable of transforming the Nature's Chaos into a Cosmos.

Only after dissecting some of its philosophical framework with the help of these stated concepts do certain symbols of the play become clear and transparent. There is, first of all, the central, all-pervading symbol of Nature, whose gigantic shadow hovers eternally over the

---

13 In the preface to his version of *Trojan Women* by Euripides. Werfel, *Gesammelte Werke, op. cit.*, pp. 546-548. This is just a paraphrase of a much longer

threatened humanity, descending upon it from time to time in order to disrupt and convulse the established, "rational" order.[14] These apocalyptic disasters may assume not only divergent shapes, but they may often cow the terrorized mass into willing victims and worshipers. The true name of these avatars, however, may not be uttered. Only Juvan, the leader and the prophet of the mutinous throng, dares to challenge during the masochistic "black mass" the deposed Greek Orthodox pope to name this living horror:

> JUVAN *(points to the royal gate)*
> Did you see him in there?
> POPE
> See? Him? Did I dare to look at him? Eh, Eh! He laughs at his bonds, the shaggy one.
> JUVAN
> And do you know who he is?
> POPE
> Do not say his name! Do not name him! You—you! Let me out! Let me out!
> JUVAN
> So you do not doubt? You believe he is what he is?
> POPE
> I believe in the death of the world. Leave me!
> JUVAN *(takes him by the throat)*
> If you believe, then name his name.
> POPE *(groaningly)*
> His given name's uprising, murder, arson, heresy. . . .[15]

There is, of course, another implication here that these "natural" destructions that occur from time to time are necessary to man not only as a warning of his inchoate and transient nature, but also as a means of clearing his decks of the past that has piled up for so long that he feels stifled under it. But if the world starts in man, this basic disjunction which exists outside of him is concurrently mirrored in man himself. ("For man is a knot, man is a cramp./Man is the animal crucified.")[16]

Argument. If we strip Werfel's ideas of tragedy of their purely theological aspect, they sound very much as if coming from the pen of any present-day dramatist.

[14] "PHYSIKUS: Auch die Menschenwelt, Freund, hat ihre leider noch nicht erforschten Jahreszeiten, Sonnenfinsternisse, Nordlichter und magnetischen Stürme. Es juckt die Ordnung. Die Urverwirrung steigt an die Oberfläche. Das verborgene Tier stößt uns auf." *Gesammelte Werke, Bocksgesang,* p. 304.

[15] *Goat Song,* trans. Langner, p. 423.   [16] *Bocksgesang,* p. 295.

Thus the monster may also simultaneously represent the symbol for the physical in man, the primitive, rendered evil by the puritanic repression accorded it by the parents.[17] They have been ashamed of the offspring of their natural love, and by confining the goat-man and regarding him as monstrous, they have made him so. For only after Mirko, their healthy son, their pride and joy, in respect to the world (thus their "Ego"), has fallen at the hands of the revolutionaries, and the monster, their shame and disgrace (their "Id"), is bared to the entire world and thus overcome, does the old couple find themselves free and happy for the first time:

STEVAN
True, father and mother are we no longer. But what are we?

MOTHER
Don't you know the word?

STEVAN *(looks at her long)*
Wife!

MOTHER *(the voice trembling)*
Husband!

STEVAN
So long since I used that word!

MOTHER *(tears streaming)*
So long . . . and where was I?

STEVAN
By my side. But awakening from all this fever I see you now, you . . . for the first time I see you again. . . .

MOTHER
Me! But I am no longer I.

STEVAN
Lovelier, lovelier, than ever I find you. The sun, the golden sun on your face—what does it matter if it is the light of your sunset.

MOTHER
You never looked at me when I was beautiful.

STEVAN
The ripened years are best. This gray on your hair— moves me, moves me so deeply.—There is something sweet and sacred about it that I cannot grasp.

[17] I am well aware that this interpretation is essentially a Freudian one. Since there was a great vogue or Freud in the twenties, it is not surprising to find that the above interpretation was widely accepted.

MOTHER *(her voice fails)*

You. . . .

STEVAN

No silver wedding will I seal with you but our second betrothal. . . . .

MOTHER *(sinks into his arms)*[18]

Dr. Marysia Turrian in her work about Werfel also points out that "the nameless monster, neither human nor beast, was born in this shape as a punishment for the sins of its parents (their lack of love)."[19]

But besides this pivotal symbol of Pan, a half human and half beast creature that populates mythologies of many countries, there is the oft encountered myth of the virgin impregnated by the god, and the miraculous conception. Here, as in many other works of Werfel, the woman becomes the chosen mediator between the divine, omnipotent and unknown forces and man lost in the quandary of his existence. And then again there is a myth of the zodiacal nature of the summer solstice, of that rare magic midnoon hour—which, by the way, holds a special fascination for Werfel—when a thing could spring from quivering nature, horrible and full of majesty, like the vision of the Whole compressed into a second.[20] The meanings and symbols continue, however, to multiply until "before long, every character has its label, its pedestal, until even the monster's younger and normal brother is a type as well as a tragedy in himself, and his parents have been blown up to the size of Erda and Adonai."[21]

And it is true that many elements of the drama such as the gnawing shame of concealment, the smug rich, the mad student, the dispossessed, and the various individuals (the rope dancer, the scavenger, etc.) are all so sharply and suggestively drawn *and* symbolized that *Goat Song* may hold one or many meanings. But the meaning of the play, or, its spiritual content, should not be sought by attempting to resolve such ambiguities as these. For even when the whole metaphysical structure is left out, the drama retains its symbolic quality and its

[18] *Goat Song,* trans. Langner, p. 430.

[19] "Das namenlose Ungeheuer, nicht Mensch und nicht Tier, kam als Strafe für die Sünden der Eltern (ihre Lieblosigkeit) in dieser Gestalt zur Welt." Dr. Marysia Turrian, *Dostojewskij und Franz Werfel,* P. Haupt Verlag, Bern, 1950, p. 81.

[20] In another of Werfel's plays, *Die Mittagsgöttin* (Goddess of Noon), the pagan goddess Mara appears and is on the height of her power in this magic noon hour. Many rituals are also connected with it.

[21] Mr. Gilbert W. Gabriel of the New York *Sun,* as quoted in the *Lit. Dig., op. cit.*

theatrical effectiveness. The scene and the locale of this "folk drama" are so expressive that Specht indicated that one received a peculiar impression from the play: "These people are speaking Slav with German words."[22] And indeed, many names of people and localities, several words and whole phrases, as well as objects and instruments used in the play appear to be quite genuine. It is true, though, that some of the names were misspelled, probably under the influence of Werfel's greater familiarity with the Czech language. Thus the diacritical mark over the letter "č" in the family names of "Milič," "Vaselič," "Trifunovič," etc., is actually supposed to be "'ć"; the student's name "Juvan" is just a somewhat corrupted form of "Jovan"; "Babka," the name of the old nurse, and "Stanjoška," the pet name of Stanja, are Russianized, due, in all probability, to Werfel's extensive reading of Dostoievsky and Turgenev at that particular period;[23] and finally, the title "Staršina" should properly be spelled "Starešina." But a far greater number of words such as: Gospodar (meaning "sir," a respectful title in addressing a man of wealth and position; Werfel must have liked this word for he also used it almost twenty-five years later in his last completed work, Star of the Unborn); Vilajet (meaning a district); Zadruga (a large family co-operative); Knez (prince, ruler, or simply a village elder), etc., belong quite properly to the locale of the play, enhancing, as it were, its authenticity. The verse recited by an old woman in Act III, scene 1 "And the prince—[Kraljevic]—wore purple-red slippers" is a line from a genuine Serbian folk ballad.[24] The mock mass, which contains some native instruments (of which the two-string Gusla is the most prominent) and the actual Church-Slavonic phrase "Pomiluj Nás Pomiluj" (meaning "Have Mercy on Us, Have Mercy on Us!"), is conducted by a strange "pope" (which simply means "priest") with a flowing, white beard and wrapped in a white, mythically fantastic chasuble. Though his name "Bogoboj" is Slav and symbolic in itself (it means "One who fears God"), he reminds one more of a Dionysian priest of ancient Greece than of an Orthodox "pope." His manner of speech and his language suggest someone who is in constant frenzy and inspired with the drunken ecstasy of the heavenly spirits:

[22] Specht, op. cit., p. 241: "Man hat den ganz merkwürdigen Eindruck: diese Menschen reden slawisch in deutschen Worten."

[23] His diaries attest to the extensive reading of Russian authors at this particular period.

[24] "Und Purpurpantoffel trug Kraljevič," alludes to the Serbian ballad cycle centered around Prince (Kraljević) Marko.

BOGOBOJ *(his eyes closed, as if in trance)*
On these clear moonlit nights they ride over the backs of
the hills and lie on the ledges, the summits, the
plateaus . . . . Oh, their hearts are trembling now with
the joy of return. They hug the trees in monstrous glee
and they listen to the pulsing sap of the pine. They
kiss the hardy blossoms of the mountain-tops and feel
bittersweet on their lips the taste of their own immor-
tality. With loving hands they fondle the fur of the
sacred untamed herds. The goats bleet and they answer
the song from the depths of their soul. *(Swaying his
head rhythmically).*
I hear in the wind the song of the goats.[25]

Though all these exotic names and phrases add to the theatrical
color of the play, they are merely external ornaments to essentially
plausible dramatic situations and some veritably incomparable human
characterization. For Werfel's *Goat Song* is, above all, a real human
drama in which the people hate, love, destroy one another, and in which
crowds swirl in anger, murder carelessly, and give themselves over to
a riot of abandoned drunkenness and lust. The individuals transcend
mere types, which make the usual expressionistic drama appear so
ponderous, and pulsate with a tremendous vitality on the stage of life.
The tragicomic Jew, ubiquitous and philosophically resigned to his
peddler role, when he, together with other dispossessed, is refused a
piece of land to settle down in the country where he was born, is a
masterfully delineated figure, repeated with virtuosity also in Werfel's
last play, *Jacobowsky and the Colonel.* When he tries to warn the rebels
that there is no joy in bloodshed nor salvation in murder, he is told:

JUVAN
Jew! Do you know why you are the lowest of all men?

FEIWEL
There is a difference of opinion about it!

JUVAN
Because you cannot understand bloodlust.

FEIWEL
Look at that! And I thought that was what made us
the chosen people.[26]

Besides some comic elements of grotesqueness which are explained by

[25] *Goat Song,* trans. Langner, pp. 409-410.
[26] *Bocksgesang,* p. 293.

the Jew's special position in the society ("In the grasp of his eternal difference"[27]), there is a great symbolic poignancy in this figure. For the Jew, it seems to be suggested, is, first of all, the stabilizer of society, standing before and after the revolution for order rather than chaos.[28] He secondly appears as this society's conscience, which, though often suppressed, could never be entirely stamped out.

Other landless vagabonds who are denied a place among the smug, wealthy proprietors are also well-characterized. Especially the vagrant American emigrant who returned to his country for nostalgic reasons is made to represent the practical aspect and interpretation of life, i.e. an "American type" from the European point of view. He talks about democracy and the War of Independence, pointing up threateningly to the example of the French Revolution. The interest in other wanderers, the gypsies, the freaks of nature who are forming a huge amorphous mass is instigated through Werfel's masterful depiction of their wild superstition.

Though most characters of the play represent types and symbols, their human reality is never put to question as it is often done in the case of the principal figure of the play who, following the well-known Werfel technique of suspense, is never directly seen on the stage.[29] One of the American critics said:

> The monster is the hovering presence which makes the
> play creepy and fills it as brimful with ominousness
> as did the relentless drum 'The Emperor Jones'—a
> thing brooding horribly over the play, but unseen save
> for one monstrous shadow thrown athwart the sun,
> unheard save for one dreadful cry out of the shadows,
> so mighty and as destroying a sound as ever I heard
> issue from human throat.[30]

While this deliberate concealment must have increased the imminent mystery of the whole play, it also diminished its ultimate reality. Werfel himself was quite conscious of this fact, for in his (unpublished) diary under the date March 21, 1922, the following entry is found: "In the

[27] "Im Zwange seiner ewigen Fremdheit," *Bocksgesang*, p. 297.
[28] This was suggested by Nathan Krass in his discourse on *Goat Song*, delivered at Temple Emanuel-el, NYC (Preserved in the New York City Public Library as a Revised Stenographic Report).
[29] This concealment of the main figure was repeated by Werfel in his play *Juarez und Maximilian*.
[30] Drama critic Woolcott of the *World*, quoted in *Lit. Dig.*, *loc. cit.*

meantime in Prague the Czech premiere of *Goat Song*. I am quite aware of the flaw of the play: the beast remains insufficiently real."[31]

The student Juvan and the girl Stanja, on the other hand, are naturalistically vivid creations, besides—in a true expressionistic sense—representing human types and abstract symbols. Juvan, the leader of the discontented, is clearly the intellectual revolutionary depicted from Werfel's own experience with the Viennese political upheaval that took place at the end of the First World War. He is a typical iconoclast who, dissatisfied with things as they are, would like to blaze the way for things that ought to be.

Werfel's greatest mastery, however, went into the creation of Stanja, the heroine of the play, another lively portrait in his remarkable gallery of women.[32] There is, no doubt, a special aura surrounding these women who often appear to be a natural link in the order of things, supernaturally empowered or burdened with unique missions. They are sometimes a necessary victim in the appeasement of cruel gods or simply an arbiter who re-establishes an upset order—human or cosmic. They can be frivolous, full of feminine wiles, or just obstinate and inquisitive, as in the case of Stanja when she inquires about the hut. To Mirko's "I'll never ask!" she replies:

> Now do you see who is the smart one? For twenty
> years you never thought or asked. But a woman
> comes to the house and asks you the first hour.[33]

But the prying, calculating Stanja of the first act soon becomes a willing sacrificial victim of an orgiastic rite, to develop finally into a passionately loving woman who is ready to die for her love. When she encounters Juvan, whom she had always loved, on his way to the execution, she realizes that their love may not be consummated even in the face of death:

[31] "Inzwischen Prag tschechische Erstaufführung "Bocksgesang." Der Fehler des Stückes ist mir ganz klar: das Tier bleibt nicht real genug." From Franz Werfel's Archives in the UCLA library (Special Collections). The diary exhibits several long gaps—and precisely in the time of the creation of *Bocksgesang*. The first mentioning of the play is on p. 50: "Gesamtgefühl—*Schweiger*—ist weniger zuversichtlich als voriges Jahr nach dem *Bocksgesang*." Above quote is on p. 58.

[32] A gallery that started with Hedwig *(Der Besuch aus Elysium),* Mara *(Die Mittagsgöttin),* Ampheh *(Spiegelmensch),* Anna *(Schweiger),* and so forth, ending with Marianne *(Jacobowsky und der Oberst),* and Io-La *(Stern der Ungeborenen).* Werfel's women are worthy of a special doctoral dissertation.

[33] *Goat Song,* trans. Langner, p. 400.

STANJA

Then tell me, mouth that is still alive, why, if we were
made for one another, it was not to be?

JUVAN

It is easy come—easy go with those who meet by chance. But
what can we do against our souls, these inexorable twins?
They implacably darken the path between them, and their
grandeur consists in their suffering.

STANJA

But why, why?

JUVAN

Because everything eternal fears fulfillment . . . .[34]

Stanja by her enigmatic feminine nature intensifies her symbolic significance. It is her irrationality (as, for example, when she willingly
submits to the beast), her unpredictability that place her on the side
with natural elements whose behavior cannot always be foreseen. It is
from her that there will be recurrence of the past, that the old order
will once more be resuscitated.

* * * * * *

It is true that symbolism in the play *Goat Song* is not always suffi-
ciently clear, and that much of it is vague and general rather than
striking and specific. It nevertheless represents one of the highest
dramatic achievements of Werfel. For, in spite of many disagreements
as to the various meanings of the play, nobody dared to deny that the
play possesses power, wonderful suggestiveness, and, above all, a high
moral and spiritual appeal. Even if we discard some of the many sec-
ondary meanings and accept only the play's central idea, i.e. Werfel's
terrifying warning that the Beast, the ghastly nightmare of humanity is
ever with us,[35] we would discover that he was here, as in his many other
works, quite prophetic. For after experiencing our recent past, it may
not at all be impossible for us to imagine a "Beast," enshrined and
worshiped with outstretched hands and frenzied cries, demanding its
innumerable human victims and laying waste to an entire continent.
It may be that Werfel's audience in the twenties refused to believe in
the possibility that such mass hysteria, madness, and destruction could
exist—except in some semibarbarous country beyond the Danube.

[34] *Bocksgesang*, p. 315.
[35] "So ist das Furchtbare unter uns; die Gefahr besteht immer, daß es sich frei
machen kann." Wilhelm Grenzmann, *Deutsche Dichtung der Gegenwart*, Menck
Verlag, Frankfurt a.M., 1953, p. 272.

GEORGE C. BUCK

The Non-Creative Prose of Franz Werfel

One of the least explored areas of Werfel research lies in the realm of non-creative prose. There have been a few paraphrases with a view to acquainting the general public with Werfel's lesser-known writings.[1] Shortly before 1933, several partisan reviewers leveled broadsides at what they regarded as propaganda hostile to the Nazi party.[2] In America Irwin Edman referred to his philosophizing as the "religiosity" illness which affects middle-aged writers who lose their nerve and despair of ever bettering civilization.[3] They usually distrust scientific method and develop a contempt for the secular world. Compared to others who have written on the same subjects, Edman says, Werfel is "amateurish" and his "shockingly confused pages" can only be regarded as "trivial intellectually." Edman's general attitude is that retreat to a mystic philosophy is basically escapist. Maynard took Werfel seriously but simply couldn't agree with him.[4] Honest efforts to understand Werfel philosophically, without interjecting personal disagreement, are rare. Articles before 1930 cannot be considered since Werfel had not yet begun to expound his philosophy in prose, otherwise we should have to include Jacobsen, Jockers, Kaufmann, and perhaps one or two others.[5] Notable among the exceptions are Klarmann, von Puttkamer, and Stamm, to name a few.[6] As yet there has not even been a systematic

[1] See W. A. Willibrand, "The Sermon-Lectures of Franz Werfel," *Books Abroad*, Autumn 1945, 350-55; and Harold von Hofe, "Literature in Exile: Franz Werfel," *German Quarterly*, XVII (Nov. 1944), 263-72.

[2] P. Haarmann, *Die Schöne Lit.*, XXXIII (1932), 315.

[3] Irwin Edman, "What Price Mysticism?" *Sat. Rev. Lit.*, XXVII, No. 27 (Nov. 18, 1944), 9 ff. [Review of *Zwischen Oben und Unten* (Between Heaven and Earth).]

[4] Theodore Maynard, *Commonweal*, XLI, No. 231 (Dec. 15, 1944), and No. 327 (Jan. 12, 1945).

[5] Anna Jacobsen, "Franz Werfel: Eine Würdigung," *Journal of English and Germanic Philology*, XXVI (1927), 337-49.

[6] Annemarie von Puttkamer, *Franz Werfel: Wort und Antwort*, Würzburg: Werkbundverlag, 1952. I. S. Stamm, "Religious Experience in Werfel's *Barbara*," *PMLA*, LIV (1939), 332-47. The publications by Klarmann are too numerous to

attempt to survey bibliographically Werfel's writing in this field.[7]

Basically, Werfel was a storyteller, a man to whom the world appeared in richly detailed and profuse images. His poetic muse never really deserted him throughout his whole life: poems appeared from his pen at the age of eighteen and did not cease until his dying day. But with the publication of *Die Troerinnen* (1915) and *Nicht der Mörder, der Ermordete ist schuldig* (1919) he was soon established in the broader fields of the drama and the novel, where his excesses were more easily tolerated than in the demanding, confining strait jacket of verse. This opinion is of course not universal. Rudolf Kayser predicted little future for Werfel in epic writing: "Werfel's writing is lyric of such intensity and compactness that any attempt at the broader epic must appear problematical. The narrative *Nicht der Mörder* . . . is not successful. Several vivid images remain . . . ."[8]

Even today with the advantage of greater distance from the subject, it is still not uncommon to discover highly divergent attitudes toward Werfel. The power of his early lyric, especially when compared with its contemporary expressionistic lyric, cannot be ignored, if one is at all objective. Yet today few would think of him primarily as a lyricist. Some would be most familiar with his dramas which number roughly a baker's dozen, though few met with great stage success. As a matter of fact, one of his greatest disappointments was the uncomprehending reception of *Spiegelmensch*, which prompted him to write an analysis of the stage, delineating his own objectives. (In so doing, he attacked Wagner, whose influence, he felt, had contributed to the stodgy attitude of both directors and critics. This naturally brought forth a storm of protests.[9]) Most people, however, would consider his most lasting achievement to be his novels and short stories.

---

mention in detail but most important is his "Franz Werfel's Eschatology and Cosmogony," *MLQ*, VII (1946), 385-410.

[7] Just as I finished this article, my colleague, Professor Reed, handed me a selective bibliography which is the most useful one to date: Claude Hill and Ralph Ley, *The Drama of German Expressionism*, A German-English Bibliography, Chapel Hill: The University of North Carolina Press, 1960. xii + 211 pp. Another specialized bibliography may be found in Herbert F. Wiese, *The Resolution of the Father-Son Conflict in the Works of Franz Werfel* (Dissertation), Univ. of Washington, 1955.

[8] Rudolf Kayser, "Franz Werfel," in *Juden in der deutschen Literatur*, ed. Gustav Krojanker, Berlin: Welt Verlag, 1922, 22.

[9] Franz Werfel, *Dramaturgie und Deutung des Zauberspiels Spiegelmensch*, Munich: Kurt Wolff Verlag, 1921.

Actually, it is surprising to note how little Werfel wrote which can properly be classed as non-creative prose. Heinz Politzer refers to the sketch "Cabrinowitsch" as a special kind of Austrian journalism which once flourished in the hands of a cultured fourth estate, but the point is that this hedging is necessary.[10] The story is essentially an eyewitness account of the famed assassin of Archduke Otto being tranported from jail to the hospital. Werfel elevates this simple incident to symbolic heights surpassing in his treatment by far what is normally understood by journalism. It is fair to point out that Werfel is not unaware of his penchant for mixing genres. In the introduction to *Zwischen Oben und Unten* (1946) he speaks of two basic literary forms which the writer has at his disposal: entertainment and confession. At which point he concludes on the apologetic note: "The reader will please forgive me for offering him at this time the second form, somewhat less mixed than usual."[11] In other words the artistic vision is primary in all his works. It is necessary to understand this thoroughly before trying to comprehend the involved and even contradictory logic of his philosophical writings. There is certainly never an intent to deceive the reader or to conceal his actual beliefs, except in the sense of his own aphorism: "Even a gifted poet or artist can reveal by concealing. And you don't think God could do the same thing?" (p. 218)[12]

No, Werfel's philosophy is not some kind of joke, nor is it the pontifical pronouncement of a self-appointed seer. Werfel may have overestimated his abilities, but there is no evidence that he was conceited or arrogant. His genuine admiration for other men is proof enough of his basic humility. Kafka, for example, was for him a "messenger of the king," and Werfel claims he always felt "conscious of the distance" between them.[13] His intensive devotion toward shaping what he felt to be a proper image of Giuseppe Verdi indicates the limits of his surrender to an ideal.[14] Sholem Asch was another who benefited from this

[10] Heinz Politzer, "Zur Prosa des jungen Franz Werfel," *Neue Rundschau,* (1949), 283.

[11] *Ibid.,* 14: "Der Leser möge es mir vergeben, daß ich ihm diesmal die zweite Form unvermischter anbiete als sonst."

[12] All quotations and page numbers within the text, unless otherwise indicated, are from *Zwischen Oben und Unten,* Stockholm: Bermann-Fischer Verlag, 1946.

[13] Franz Werfel, "Recollections," *The Kafka Problem,* ed. Angel Flores, New York: New Directions, 1946, 39.

[14] *Giuseppe Verdi Briefe,* editing and Introduction by Franz Werfel, Berlin: Paul Zsolnay Verlag, 1926.

kindly but penetrating gaze.[15] There is every evidence that the poet earnestly sought the cosmic answers to his spiritual problems, regardless of the limitations to his abilities which may be ascribed to him by others. In a volume of portraits and self-portraits of famous people, Werfel in a single paragraph etches his goal with remarkable candor in a choice of words which, however, would evoke a dubious response from some of his readers. "My lifework," he says, "is to be objective and to formulate ideas but not to chat idly about myself."[16] If this statement can be taken seriously, and I can see no reason to ignore it, it is up to us to attempt to *interpret* his meaning, rather than to reject it in its entirety because it does not conform to standards imposed from without. It is often too true that calling a person's ideas meaningless means simply that the name-caller has failed to understand them, either because he is incapable of doing so or because he did not make the effort.

In all, Werfel has written scarcely two dozen essays which could properly be considered within the scope of our topic. It was not possible to verify and read each one of these items, largely for bibliographical reasons. The early essays are quite difficult to locate and some are as yet not accessible. Some hint as to the nature of the first publications is available in the commentated bibliography of Specht. In the writings of Professors Klarmann, Arlt, and von Hofe there are many references to unpublished materials, but valuable information still remains scanty. In spite of this, it could still be maintained with reasonable confidence that everything of significance as far as the broader picture of Werfel is concerned can be found in the one volume *Zwischen Oben und Unten* (1946), which I shall discuss briefly.

Essentially, the book is composed of three essays and a collection of aphorisms, the latter published here for the first time. The first two essays were delivered in a somewhat abridged form throughout the length and breadth of Germany, immediately prior to the Nazi accession to power, when political speeches of such persuasion could be pretty risky business indeed. As a matter of fact, Werfel relates in the introduction how a prejudiced group of students in Insterburg, East Prussia, booed and catcalled him out of the hall under a clearly unsympathetic police protection. The fact that he dared deliver such speeches in the face of such obvious hostility, in what is reported to be a brilliant plat-

15 Address before the P.E.N. Club in Vienna.
16 "Franz Werfel" in *Portraits and Self Portraits*, ed. George Schreiber, Boston: Houghton Mifflin Co., 1936, 139.

form manner, testifies to the firmness of his convictions. This fact alone should justify our attention to his message.

The two early speeches, "Realismus und Innerlichkeit"[17] (1931) and "Können wir ohne Gottesglauben leben?"[18] (1932) seek to explore the historical, economic, psychological, and metaphysical roots of our modern society. A third speech, "Von der reinsten Glückseligkeit des Menschen"[19] (1938), assesses the role of the arts in this society and the dangers which beset them. The style of all three essays is not that of a carefully wrought, closely reasoned treatise on logic, but rather a loose, haphazard, and often whimsical selection of impressions, recollections, and interpretations, woven together with great emotional force into a pattern of persuasive imagery. The last half of the book is a collection of maxims and reflections in the Goethean sense of the word, written in series around central topics. They contain nothing which might be called "new" in Werfel's cosmogony, but they do furnish analogies to more precise definitions of themes which occur elsewhere: e.g. the nature of sin, Judaism, and the problems of conversion, incarnation, etc.

In the first essay, "Realismus und Innerlichkeit" (1930), Europe, formerly the proud cultural leader of the world, is reduced to a helpless · victim squeezed between the jaws of giant pincers: one arm representing Russian communism and the other, American behaviourism. Both however are forms of what he terms "radical realism." Such pressure is bound to have effect, regardless of the cultural strength of the prisoner. But what choice is open?

Communism, on the one hand, explains society as a product of economic dynamics. The "soul" of the "pre-scientific" world is simply the psychological superstructure. The inner life is hence completely determined—a by-product as it were of the economic chemistry. Once man has succeeded in controlling the economic factors, the spiritual problems in this classless society would disappear automatically. In essence, this is a collective approach toward the control of suffering and the attainment of happiness.

Werfel was not born in the shadow of behaviourism, as he was in the case of Communism, and hence his hesitance is understandable. Though he does express a few opinions, he is quick to state they are hearsay and that he hopes to complete and verify his knowledge shortly

[17] "Realism and Inwardness."
[18] "Can We Live Without Faith in God?"
[19] "Of Man's True Happiness."

during a projected visit to the United States. John B. Watson had published his book *Behaviourism* in 1925, and this is taken as typical of the
general American philosophy, in the absence of any official dogma.
Under this concept man becomes simply a puppet, dependent on two
basic drives of love and death. Education can teach him how to act and
react so the social order can progress without danger. Such a belief,
Werfel feels, explains the conformity of both clothing and opinion typical of Americans, according to reports of his friends.

The chief difficulty in trying to understand this essay arises if you
insist on a clear line of reasoning. The title patently establishes a tension
between realism and inwardness. (Heinz Politzer has pointed out the
almost uncanny comprehensiveness and aptness of all Werfel's titles.)
It is the first half of the equation which lacks clear definition. At one
place reality is the "direct relation to the thing(s) of life, the most
unprejudiced relationship to nature, uncolored by religious, political
or other abstractions" (p. 23). Yet it is not apparent whether Werfel
would feel this to be "good" or "bad." After all, realism did lead to the
brilliant nineteenth century of Zola, Balzac, Dostoievski, Tolstoi,
Manet, and others, as he points out. And if I have understood him cor-
rectly, it would be a fairly close description of his prehistoric man who
also comprehended reality directly and was certainly unhampered by
religious, political, or other abstractions. We have come a long way
from the "noble savage," but it has not all been progress, if Werfel is
right. Somewhere in his cosmic vision reality breaks down into "radical
realism," or as he later terms it "naturalistic nihilism," but nowhere, to
my knowledge, is the dividing line clearly defined.

In an attempt to clarify this issue for myself I have tried to state the
ideal situation which Werfel may have had in mind, though I cannot
claim any special insight. The *radical* realist apprehends reality directly,
accepts, as it were, only those facts furnished him through his physical
senses and his education. Objects and experiences do not cause him to
reflect or entertain their various potentialities. Rather, he assigns them
single, ultimate values from a utilitarian point of view. The "mentalist,"
or person blessed by the muses, perceives reality historically or as a
totality. He reflects, relates his knowledge and experience to the immediate, and vice versa. Thus words and objects acquire "extra" values
for the poetic nature. In this way our lives are expanded and enriched.
It is in effect converting external reality to inner experience, which
Werfel later defines as complete happiness.

One of Werfel's favorite devices is the paradoxical axiom which occurs frequently in the essays. "Reality," he says, "decreases quadratically with the degree of perfection of its technical advances" (p. 26). The significance of this statement is most clearly seen in the lives of a farmer and a modern worker in an electronics factory. The farmer is still able to oversee his total operation and comprehend each of its parts. The city-dwelling worker whirls into work by subway, rapid suburban train, or threads his way through a maze of interlocking highways to a job so minute and specific that it consists of only a few prescribed motions whose sole reward is a certain amount of buying power (ironically enough, used to buy what he doesn't need). The worker himself has no concept of what he is doing in relation to the whole. Thus the realist or materialist is in actuality living a most unreal life. This situation began with the French revolution and has grown progressively worse. The mass planning, which is necessary for such a life, is gradually destroying individualism. The realistic attitude which results therefrom is forced to make new evaluations. Each evaluation in turn produces a fanatical aggression, whose natural object of hate is the inwardness of man, his soul, the creative spirit. This hatred is of double origin: (a) the Luciferian-Promethean drive in man to make this world autonomous is an eternal metaphysical urge; and (b) the feelings of inferiority on the part of "cultureless" peoples or classes who are physically victorious over these "superior" classes represents the temporal-historical cause.

This whole development is explained psychologically by the need of man for a tangible ideal, powerful enough to justify his personal sacrifice, to replace the lost core of medieval society. The heroic-knightly ideal lies far beyond the reach of the modest little shopkeeper, and the ascetic-religious ideal exercises no appeal. He is unable to comprehend the fact that all intellectual activity requires leisure, or in his eyes "idleness." The social stratum substituted for these outmoded ideals the concept of *work* as the only valid yardstick or moral accomplishment. Such an ideal requires no great courage or personal sacrifice to uphold, *and* it produces bread. It was responsible for bringing about enormous changes in an unbelievably short time. It is, however, hostile to intellectual creativity. (Unfortunately, Werfel did not live to see the "egghead" or esthete redeemed—albeit in the limited sphere of science.) The example Werfel uses to depict a more satisfactory situation is, I'm afraid, a highly idealized picture of German intellectual society a few

centuries ago, pursuing its threadbare existence but satisfied with the
assurance of rich inner rewards. Since World War I realism has accom-
plished the intimidation and suppression of human inwardness and the
devaluation of the creative spirit. The soul has been deprived of faith.
The new goal is making the unnecessary necessary. (Just look at the
American advertising industry to see the validity of this insight. You
could even supplement it with personal experiences, based on any one
of the dozens of American fads.) The new virtues are activism, faith
in progress, and efficiency.[20]

As mottoes for his second essay, Werfel has selected two quotations.
Fritz Mauthner writes on "Gott" in the *Philosophisches Wörterbuch:*
"Es gibt wichtigere Fragen."[21] And from Isaiah: "Wächter, wie weit in
der Nacht?"[22] The first seems to contain modern man's attitude to the
question whether we can live without faith in God. The second em-
bodies Werfel's feeling of directionlessness. Several times he uses
images which underscore our inability to discern even the slightest
degree of orientation. One is the leaf on an eddying current which can
have no concept of progress or regress. He makes fun of books with
such titles as "The Rise of . . ."; "The Decline and Fall . . .," indicating
that our relatively short period of recorded history is not sufficient basis
on which to posit theories of progress, in the face of our billions of years
of existence. He even indulges in the fantasy that there may have been
more advanced civilizations than our own.

In the appended summary to this speech, Werfel introduces four
categories of proof for the existence of God. Psychological: Cults, rites,
dogma, documents, and personal testimony proclaiming inner perception of the divine can all be denied individually, but not the experience
which generated them. Reasonable: Making sense out of the world by
human thought processes depends on sense and consequence, pre-
requisites of which are a first and final sense. Moral: The value of the
world is realized through man. Naturalistic nihilism claims human
morality is a denial of the instincts. The theory that we have only two
drives of lust and aggression would lead ultimately to murder or suicide, since few enjoy standing still. Esthetic: Taking a principle from
mathematics, where the neater of two correct solutions is usually pre-

[20] It should be noted that when materialism and militarism gained full sway,
the poet Krasny in *Barbara* was unable to exist any longer.
[21] "There are more important questions."
[22] "Watchman, how far in the night?"

ferred, he says, if truth is not decisive, beauty is. Between a God-less and a God-filled world, the latter is certainly the prettier solution.

None of these are in themselves convincing arguments but they are emotionally appealing to the receptive. This analysis of our metaphysical plight shows how science furnished the tools to sever our lines to a metaphysical anchor. But we need these ties ("re-ligio") back to something solid and comforting. World War I left only a void which became filled in many instances by surrogate religions. Nihilism reached its final development with the end of that war, when man, having been stripped of all faith, was left with only his naked ego. With nothing to live for, he fell easy prey to communism and nationalism, both of which incidentally are rooted in dogmatic belief, not in intellectual soil, as they like to claim. Communism debases intellectual life to a function of the social situation. Literature under such conditions becomes merely an opiate to keep the proletariat from awakening. Nationalism commits an even greater sin by elevating the accident of biological origin to the imposing heights of a *moral value.* It demands less of the citizen and offers less. The goals of both these surrogate religions are technology and the state. Ghostly irreality prevails, individualism is destroyed. The realist can only live from birth to death, trying to make the best of a senseless existence.

Only in the knowledge of an eternal perfection, however, can we become aware of our own imperfection. And only the conviction of the transcendental importance in each moment of time can bring us to the realization that life can be given direction and purpose. We become aware of our guilt.[23] This sacred feeling transports us to the state of reverence (reminiscent of Goethe's three states of reverence), where it transforms social and national communities of interest into a genuine brotherhood of man, sexuality into love, which in turn transfigures marriage and procreation from unpleasant accident to the adoration of the child. Finally, even death is transformed so that we are no longer going from nothing to nothing. Death loses its frightening aspects, and life its bestial seriousness. The result is something resembling Schiller's *Spieltrieb* (creative drive). The arts flourish only where there is security, naiveté, and the sense of continuity.

Since the Renaissance we have been slipping backwards into this

---

[23] From a study of the MS of *Stern der Ungeborenen,* Klarmann is able to point out that Werfel substitued *contrite guilt* for another motif as the most incisive moment in F. W's life, See *MLQ,* VII (1946), 388, n. 9.

state of nihilism. Even as a Jew, Werfel feels justified in proclaiming our only salvation lies on the road to a genuine Christianity. The tremendous possibilities latent in this religion of selfless love have not even been dreamed of as yet. Human life is just not possible without a transcendant alliance. Atheism, he feels, arises not from an insight but from the wish that God does not exist and is itself a kind of perverted belief in God. The principle of Christianity is to "live against one's own wishes for truth and life." (p. 122) The goal of such a life is joy. Looking at the problem negatively, if we assume that man among all the animals happened to use his brain as a weapon to survive, it would mean the intellectual products: works of art, Plato, philosophies, etc., owe their existence to mere chance, and that is hard to believe.

The final essay, "Von der reinsten Glückseligkeit des Menschen," was a speech delivered in Vienna in 1937, published in 1938. Its chief concern really centers in the arts and the artist. Once again, Werfel mildly challenges Darwin's theory, but this is in all probability not to be taken too seriously. The mystic belief in the "noble savage" who speaks only in images, which would reveal a direct comprehension of the divine secrets if we could only check on them, plays a significant part here too. A somewhat strange proof is offered in the Babylonian epic *Gilgamesh*.[24] But this again is the esthete out of his depth: Goethe trying to combat Newton's theory of optics with psychological arguments instead of mathematical ones.

When the esthete Werfel concentrates on his own field, he becomes much more interesting for us. Since Aristotle's "fear" and "pity," the function of the arts has been a hotly contested subject. We, as human beings, have come a long way from the "noble savage." Our progress has been cyclical. The economic and social progress is always reflected in the arts. In every great work of art Werfel sees a lofty theological symbolism. Here too the artistic peaks are marked by religion and symbolism, the valleys by realism and naturalism. Realism is the sign of an old and decaying culture. In some way he links this with the physical cycle in man, who turns his sexual energies, thwarted and stultified after fifty, to the economic aspects of life. (Very old men, however, ap-

[24] The reason given for our being almost unable to understand the Babylonian epic lies in the countless number of "cosmic-astral meanings" which we can no longer fathom. Actually, we are in possession of only 1,500 lines of an estimated 3,500. Instead of the original one language and 12 large tablets, we have 3 languages and about 30,000 different tablets.

proach once more the "genius" of childhood.) The modern realist no longer believes in a spiritual creation but in a materialistic-economic beginning and end. The goal of life is to achieve the highest possible degree of earthly comfort. This alone will lead us to the Golden Age. On this point all political idealogies, no matter how disparate, are in agreement. This is the extreme limit of disbelief. Proof of this despair of life may be found not in the suicide rate, but in the fanatic striving for amusement, sun-worshiping, skin-diving, spectator sports—all forms of time-wasting. The arts, on the other hand, paradoxical though it may seem, attempt to halt time in its flight. History halts only the specific moment but the arts aim at total recall.

The goal of the poet is to wake man from his anxiety neurosis and to draw him away from material things. Realistic art (forced upon the artist in the totalitarian countries) serves no purpose. The true artist elevates what he sees around him to a vision, which alone is capable of revealing the fact and investing it with a poetic quality. A final definition of happiness is the ability of each of us to develop the spiritual powers, latent within us. The artist alone can furnish the key.

The final half of the book entitled *Theologumena* (written 1942-44) contains much the same material in a different form. One thing is immediately apparent. The aphorism, as a poetic genre, is less bald, more opaque, more suggestive than oratorical persuasion. It requires the reader to think through the poet's vision. It demands engagement and allows commitment. The oratorical prose repels or attracts. It would be interesting to compare the specific views maintained by Werfel in these writings with their artistic echoes in the creative works, where they are probably much more convincing to the average reader.

Werfel selected a quotation from Goethe as motto for his book to the effect that there is only one real theme in the whole history of mankind, the conflict of belief and disbelief. All of Werfel's non-creative prose can be viewed from this point of view. Seen as a totality, it is a sincere documentary of empassioned commitment to a morally responsible life. It is not, as some have said, a capitulation to the realistic man of action. Werfel has failed to bring out the positive features of his vision as sharply as the negative criticism—at least not in terms which the realist understands, but nevertheless, the message is there for those who will hear it. He does demand the full utilization of our native gifts under conscious consideration for all human beings. His

views fit in the long tradition of the artist as seer and prophet which
perhaps has found more acceptance in Germany than elsewhere. We
of today tend to be skeptical of the non-professional. Goethe and
Thomas Mann, who have also engaged in this kind of endeavor, did
manage to achieve a relatively high degree of competence in the chosen
medium. Here Werfel is disappointing, and yet there is a warm and
kindly heart beating out a message which deserves a sympathetic
audience, rather than a coldly professional snub.[25]

[25] Without disturbing the structure of this article I should like to call attention
to a most remarkable contrast which haunted me at every turn.

Rudolf Borchardt (1877-1945) is only 13 years older than Werfel, though
they died in the same year. Each had his origin in the Eastern empire and came
of Jewish stock. In Borchardt's case the conversion from Judaism to Lutheranism
took place some 150 years before the poet's birth, according to his own testimony.
Yet many stories bear witness to his sensitivity about his religion. Werfel became fully convinced in the course of his life that Catholicism was the only true
religion, although as a Jew, he himself would betray his holy mission were he
to embrace that faith. Only through the witness of the Jew and his eternal per-
secution is the truth of the Messiah attested. Although Werfel wrestled with this
problem all his life, his well-adjusted personality seems to have been able to
reconcile himself to his own solution with no apparent embarrassment. A hostile
critic might take the point of view that Werfel's many attempts to justify and
even glorify the role of the Jew in the world derives at least in part from a deep-
seated guilt. And yet who doesn't attempt to justify himself? As a matter of fact,
this very guilt becomes a cardinal force in all our lives under Werfel's concept,
as we have seen.

Borchardt's first poems were published at 19 in a private edition. He appar-
ently wrote and destroyed many more even before that. The Zehn Gedichte
(1896) have as yet not been included in the collected works for some strange
reason. Even though they do show marked traces of a derivative nature, they
also harbor traits which were to stay with B. all his life, e.g. his constant in-
fatuation with perfection on form and sound, sometime to the detriment of
meaning.

Werfel on the other hand had his first poems ferreted out of his possession by
an admiring student and sent in to Die Zeit (Wien) when he was only 18. This
same Willy Haas, incidentally, was one of the early admirers of B. though the
relationship was not nearly as pleasant. Precocity, ease of publication, public
acclamation, and prolificity mark all Werfel's subsequent years. Borchardt's private printings containing several fragments which were never completed, though
often promised, symbolize his further development. Much of his publication
reached only an extremely limited audience and then only through the graces of
wealthy sponsors who saw a great potential going to waste. Werfel's first great
success was a volume of poetry entitled Der Weltfreund. This apt title could
easily be applied to the whole of Werfel, man and work. If I were asked to pro-
duce a similar title for Borchardt, it would probably be "Der Weltfeind," to
properly catch the brittle, hostile, almost majestic arrogance which often speaks
from his writings, especially his non-creative prose—if such a distinction can be
made at all.

Only once did Werfel feel impelled to resort to prose in order to clarify his intentions, when the critics exhibited their consternation and bewilderment at the appearance of *Der Spiegelmensch.* Borchardt's initial hurt at the publication of *Das Buch Joram* (1907) led him to deliver a justifying lecture before a public reading in Munich some four years later. Nearly all his major works were accompanied by an epilogue of brilliantly fashioned scholarship, revealing a keen awareness of the problems involved.

If we look at some of the themes which interested both authors, we are again struck with the similarity. Both were disappointments to their mercantile fathers, but Werfel's ameliorating friendliness did not suffer any out and out breach, whereas B. left home in his early twenties and never saw his father again, though he was trying to bring about a reconciliation just as his father died. Yet when we look for this theme in his works, it appears only in disguise. In *Joram* old Pinchas, representing the traditional heathen beliefs, is rejected in a kindly way by his son Joram who refuses to employ the usual "Letter of Separation" to free himself from a beloved but barren wife. (Yet this is very probably one of the reasons for his ultimate separation from his first wife, intimated in the lines "Das Land hat keine Kinder und kein Licht. / Das Feld erstickt im Korn, doch reift es nicht.") In *Die Beichte des Bocchino Belforti* (written 1904; published 1923), the teenage Bocchino assumes a direct fealty relationship with his Lord and resents anyone hearing his final confession but the Archbishop. His final thanks to the Lord for his parents "Messer Filippo" and "Monna Narda" is sharply undercut by the sheepish admission somewhat later that his father was the non-warrior in the family, a modest man, an unimportant innkeeper with a knowledge of book-keeping. There are other explanations for this which I hope to publish shortly, but it is not impossible that this description is colored to some extent by the image of his tea-merchant father who went over to the banking business.

The problem is somewhat more blurred in *Der Durant* ([1904] 1920). Here the father, off to the Holy Land, leaves his son with an uncle who assumes the role of the tolerant father, familiar to him after raising ten sons. Durant's problem is "sibling" rivalry with the perfectly mannered Hardwin, oldest of the sons, in an attempt to secure the admiration and respect of all. Nowhere is the clash of the generations basic.

The problem which did interest both authors is that of sin-guilt-penance-atonement-salvation. It is basic to all four of Borchardt's narratives. Three have already been mentioned. The fourth, *Die halbgerettete Seele,* is esthetically the most satisfactory. There is no point in pursuing the analogy further. It was my intention to show the irreconcilable polarity between what might have been identical molds.

FRANK McGOWAN

Bibliography, Works Published 1911-1950

The bibliography includes monographs and separately published works, but not works published in periodicals. It aims to be complete through 1950 and it contains Werfel's own poems, plays, novels, and essays in the original German and in English translation as well as his work as translator and editor. Because of the ready availability of works published since 1950, it has not been thought necessary to include later editions.

Works by Franz Werfel

1911   *Der Weltfreund. Erste Gedichte.* Leipzig: K. Wolff. 116 pp.

1912   *Der Weltfreund. Gedichte.* Berlin: K. Wolff. 116 pp.

1913   "Das Opfer," in *Arkadia. Ein Jahrbuch für Dichtkunst.* Leipzig.
       Die Versuchung. Ein Gespräch des Dichters mit dem Erzengel und Luzifer. Leipzig: K. Wolff. 31 pp. (Der Jüngste Tag, Bd. I)
       Wir sind. Neue Gedichte. Leipzig: K. Wolff. 127 pp.

1915   *Einander. Oden, Lieder, Gestalten.* Leipzig, München: K. Wolff. 107 pp.

1917   *Gesänge aus den drei Reichen. Ausgew. Gedichte.* Leipzig, München: K. Wolff. 110 pp. (Der Jüngste Tag, Bd. XXIX-XXX)
       Die Versuchung. Ein Gespräch des Dichters .... 2. Aufl. Leipzig: K. Wolff. 32 pp.

1918   *Der Weltfreund. Erste Gedichte.* Leipzig: K. Wolff. 114 pp.

1919   "Der Dschin." "Ein Märchen." "Der Gerichtstag." "Blasphemie eines Irren." "Fragmente." Leipzig: O. Klemm. 32 pp. *(Daimon; eine Monatsschrift)*
       Der Gerichtstag. In 5 Büchern. Leipzig, München: K. Wolff. 309 pp.

1920   *Der Besuch aus dem Elysium. Romantisches Drama in einem Aufzug.* München: K. Wolff. 23 pp.

Nicht der Mörder, der Ermordete ist schuldig. Eine Novelle. München: K. Wolff. 269 pp.

Spiegelmensch. Magische Trilogie. München: K. Wolff. 223 pp.

1921   *Bocksgesang. In 5 Akten.* München: K. Wolff. 160 pp.

1922   *Arien.* München: K. Wolff. 43 pp.

Schweiger. Ein Trauerspiel in 3 Akten. München: K. Wolff. 155 pp.

1923   *Beschwörungen.* München: K. Wolff. 104 pp.

Die Mittagsgöttin. Ein Zauberspiel. München: K. Wolff. 75 pp. (Dichtungen Bd. VI). Ursprünglich als 2. Teil des 4. Buches des Werkes "'Der Gerichtstag" erschienen.

1924   *Juarez und Maximilian. Dramatische Historie in 3 Phasen und 13 Bildern.* Berlin: Zsolnay. 195 pp.

Verdi. Roman der Oper. Berlin: Zsolnay. 570 pp.

1925   *Verdi: A Novel of the Opera.* New York: Simon and Schuster. 438 pp.

1926   *Goat Song (Bocksgesang): A drama in five acts.* The Theatre Guild version. Garden City, N. Y.: Doubleday, Page. 161 pp.

Juarez and Maximilian: A dramatic history in three phases and thirteen pictures. Theatre Guild version. New York: Simon and Schuster. 160 pp.

Die Macht des Schicksals. Leipzig: G. Ricordi. 101 pp. (Freely adapted from the Italian,"La Forza del Destino," of F. M. Piave)

Paulus unter den Juden. Dramat. Legende in 6 Bildern. Wien: Zsolnay. 187 pp.

Verdi: A novel of the opera. London: Jarrolds. 384 pp.

1927   *Death of a Poor Man.* London: Benn. 186 pp.

Gedichte. Berlin: Zsolnay. 467 pp.

Geheimnis eines Menschen. Novellen. Wien: Zsolnay. 316 pp.

The Man Who Conquered Death. New York: Simon and Schuster. 134 pp.

1928   *Der Abituriententag. Die Geschichte einer Jugendschuld.* Wien: Zsolnay. 325 pp.

      Paul Among the Jews: A tragedy. London: Diocesan House. 150 pp.

      Der Tod des Kleinbürgers. Novelle. Wien: Zsolnay. 112 pp.

1929   *Der Abituriententag. Die Geschichte einer Jugendschuld.* Wien: Zsolnay. Neue Ausgabe. 335 pp.

      Barbara; oder Die Frömmigkeit. Wien: Zsolnay (Ausg. 1931). 808 pp.

      Class Reunion. New York: Simon and Schuster. 204 pp.

      Gesammelte Werke. Wien: Zsolnay. 7 Bde. (Barbara, Dramatische Dichtung, Die Troerinnen, Juarez und Maximilian, Paulus unter den Juden, Gedichte [1927])

      Simone Boccanegra. Lyrische Tragödie in einem Vorspiel und drei Akten. Leipzig, 1929. 84 pp. (Freely adapted from the Italian of F. M. Piave)

1930   *Death of a Poor Man.* London: Benn. 192 pp.

      Gesammelte Werke. Wien: Zsolnay. (Barbara, Die 40 Tage des Musa Dagh)

      Das Reich Gottes in Böhmen. Tragödie eines Führers. Wien: Zsolnay. 207 pp.

      "Der Tod des Kleinbürgers," in *Neue deutsche Erzähler.* Berlin: P. Franke. Vol. 4.

1931   *Der Gerichtstag. In 5 Büchern.* Wien: Zsolnay. 234 pp.

      Die Geschwister von Neapel. Wien: Zsolnay. 498 pp.

      Hidden Child. London: Jarrolds. 610 pp. (Published in New York under the title *Pure in Heart*)

      Juarez und Maximilian. Dramatische Historie. Mit Einleitung und Anmerkungen für den Schulgebrauch von Paul Jacob. Wien: Zsolnay. 194 pp.

      Kleine Verhältnisse. Wien: Zsolnay. 111 pp.

      The Pure in Heart. New York: The Book League of America. 610 pp.

      The Pure in Heart. New York: Simon and Schuster. 610 pp.

      Realismus und Innerlichkeit (Flammender Aufruf des großen Dichters. Rede). Wien: Zsolnay, 35 pp.

1932   *Das Geheimnis des Saverio.* Leipzig: Reclam. 68 pp.

Können wir ohne Gottesglauben leben? (Reden und Schriften).
Wien: Zsolnay. 72 pp.

Pascarella Family. London: Jarrolds. 383 pp.

The Pascarella Family. New York: Simon and Schuster. 437 pp.

1933   *Barbara; oder Die Frömmigkeit.* Wien: Zsolnay. 808 pp. (edited
but not condensed)

Hidden Child. London: Jarrolds. 584 pp.

Realismus und Innerlichkeit. Berlin: Zsolnay. 37 pp.

Die vierzig Tage des Musa Dagh. Roman. Wien: Zsolnay. 2 vols.

1934   *The Forty Days.* London: Jarrolds. 653 pp.

The Forty Days of Musa Dagh. New York: Viking. 824 pp.

1935   *Schlaf und Erwachen. Neue Gedichte.* Wien: Zsolnay. 130 pp.

Der Weg der Verheißung. Ein Bibelspiel. Wien: Zsolnay. 127 pp

1936   *The Eternal Road: A drama in four parts.* New York: Viking.
144 pp.

1937   *In einer Nacht. Ein Schauspiel.* Wien: Zsolnay. 109 pp.

The Eternal Road: A drama in four parts. London: Jarrolds.
146 pp. (limited autograph edition)

————. Toronto: Ryerson Press, 1937. 146 pp.

The Forty Days. London: Jarrolds. 653 pp.

————. Toronto: Ryerson Press. 653 pp.

The Forty Days of Musa Dagh. New York: Modern Library.
824 pp.

Höret die Stimme. Wien: Zsolnay. 755 pp. (Gesammelte Werke)

Twilight of a World. New York: Viking. 692 pp.

————. London: Jarrolds. 611 pp.

1938   *Hearken unto the Voice.* London: Jarrolds. 588 pp.

————. New York: Viking. 780 pp.

Jeremias. Höret die Stimme. Frankfurt a.M.: S. Fischer. 552 pp.

Twilight of a World. London: Jarrolds. 611 pp. (cheaper edition)

Von der reinsten Glückseligkeit des Menschen. Stockholm:
Bermann-Fischer. 50 pp.

1939 *Gedichte aus dreißig Jahren.* Stockholm: Bermann-Fischer. 251 pp.

 Hearken unto the Voice. London: Jarrolds. 592 pp.

 Der veruntreute Himmel. Die Geschichte einer Magd. Stockholm: Bermann-Fischer. 414 pp.

 Die vierzig Tage des Musa Dagh. Roman. Amsterdam: Forum. 2 Bde.

1940 *Embezzled Heaven.* London: Hamilton. 350 pp.

 ————. New York: Viking. 427 pp.

1941 *Eine blaßblaue Frauenschrift.* Buenos Aires: Editorial Estrellas. 155 pp.

 Das Lied von Bernadette. Stockholm: Bermann-Fischer. 559 pp.

1942 *Embezzled Heaven.* Garden City, N. Y.: Sun Dial Press. 427 pp.

 The Song of Bernadette. New York: Viking. 575 pp.

 ————. London: Hamilton. 575 pp.

 Die wahre Geschichte vom wiederhergestellten Kreuz. Los Angeles: Privatdruck der Pazifischen Presse. 49 pp.

1943 *Das Lied von Bernadette.* London: Hamilton. 506 pp.

 Paul Among the Jews. London: Grey Walls Press. 80 pp.

 The Song of Bernadette, New York: Viking. 404 pp.

 ————. Melbourne: Jaboor. 397 pp.

1944 *Between Heaven and Earth.* New York: Philosophical Library. 252 pp.

 ————. London: Hutchinson. 176 pp.

 Jacobowsky and the Colonel. New York: Random House. 177 pp.

 ————. New York: Viking. 120 pp.

 Jakobowsky und der Oberst. Komödie einer Tragödie in drei Akten. Stockholm: Bermann-Fischer. 129 pp.

 The Song of Bernadette. Garden City, N. Y.: Sun Dial Press. 575 pp.

 ————. Toronto: Macmillan. 575 pp.

 ————. Indian ed. Calcutta: Thacker and Co. 575 pp.

 The Song of Bernadette: A Play in three acts, dramatized from the novel, by Jean and Walter Kerr. Chicago: Dramatic Publishing Company. 101 pp.

Verdi: A novel of the opera. London: Jarrolds. 192 pp. (cheaper edition)

1945 *Embezzled Heaven: A play in a prologue and three acts.* Adapted by Laszló Bus-Fekete and M. H. Fay. New York: Viking. 100 pp.

⸻⸻⸻. Toronto: Macmillan. 100 pp.

Jacobowsky und der Oberst. Komödie einer Tragödie in 3 Akten. ed. with introductory notes and vocabulary by Gustave O. Arlt. New York: Crofts. 208 pp.

⸻⸻⸻. Stockholm: Bermann-Fischer. 141 pp.

Poems. Princeton: University Press. 119 pp.

1946 *Gedichte aus den Jahren 1908-1945.* Hrsg. von Ernst Gottlieb und Felix Guggenheim. Los Angeles: Pazifische Presse. 167 pp.

Die Geschwister von Neapel. Stockholm: Bermann-Fischer. 403 pp.

Poems. Oxford: University Press. 119 pp.

Star of the Unborn. New York: Viking. 645 pp.

Stern der Ungeborenen. Ein Reiseroman. Stockholm: Bermann-Fischer. 659 pp.

⸻⸻⸻. Wien: Bermann-Fischer. 714 pp.

Zwischen oben und unten. Stockholm: Bermann-Fischer. 369 pp.

1947 *Between Heaven and Earth.* London: Hutchinson. 176 pp.

Die Kämpfe der Schwachen. Aus dem Roman "Die vierzig Tage des Musa Dagh." Wien: Grobus-Verlag. 109 pp.

Verdi: A novel of the opera. New York: Allen, Towne & Heath. 438 pp.

⸻⸻⸻. Toronto: McLeod. 438 pp.

Die vierzig Tage des Musa Dagh. Stockholm: Bermann-Fischer. 2 Bde.

1948 *Der Abituriententag.* ed. Gustave O. Arlt. New York: Rinehart. 249 pp.

Erzählungen aus zwei Welten. Erster Band: Krieg und Nachkrieg. Stockholm: Bermann-Fischer. 297 pp.

Krieg und Nachkrieg. Amsterdam, etc.: Bermann-Fischer. 297 pp. (Gesammelte Werke)

Das Lied von Bernadette. Wien: Bermann-Fischer. 559 pp.

Schönste Gedichte. Für die Freunde gedruckt. Leipzig (Werkstätten der Akademie für Graphik und Buchkunst). 14 pp.

Der veruntreute Himmel. Die Geschichte einer Magd. Amsterdam: Bermann-Fischer. 360 pp.

Der veruntreute Himmel . . . . Wien: Bermann-Fischer. 450 pp.

1949 *Stern der Ungeborenen. Ein Reiseroman.* Berlin: Suhrkamp. 714 pp. (Gesammelte Werke)

Verdi. Roman der Oper. Wien, etc.: Bermann-Fischer. 524 pp. (Gesammelte Werke)

1950 *Die Geschwister von Neapel.* Frankfurt a.M., etc.: S. Fischer. 426 pp. (Gesammelte Werke)

Das Lied von Bernadette. Berlin, etc.: Suhrkamp. 412 pp.

Musa Dagh und Bernadette nebst anderen Romanfragmenten. Hrsg. von J. H. Schonten. Groningen: Wolters. 158, 15 pp.

Translations and Editions

1915 Euripides. *Die Troerinnen (Troades).* In deutscher Bearbeitung von Franz Werfel. Leipzig, München: K. Wolff. 127 pp.

1916 ⸺. 119 pp.

1920 ⸺. Nach der Tragödie des Euripides. München: K. Wolff. 133 pp.

1926 Verdi, Giuseppe. *Briefe,* hrsg. u. eingel. von Franz Werfel. Übers. von Paul Stefan. Wien: P. Zsolnay. 392 pp.

1929 Verdi, Giuseppe. *Simone Boccanegra. Lyrische Tragödie in einem Vorspiel und drei Akten.* Leipzig, New York: Ricordi. 84 pp.

1950 Verdi, Giuseppe. *Die Macht des Schicksals. Oper in einem Vorspiel u. 3 Akten.* Dem Ital. des F. M. Piave frei nachgedichtet u. f. d. deutsche Opernbühne bearb. von Franz Werfel. Neuaufl. Mailand: Ricordi. 67 pp.